OPEN WOUNDS

Human Rights Abuses in Kosovo

Human Rights Watch/Helsinki
(Formerly Helsinki Watch)

Human Rights Watch
New York • Washington • Los Angeles • London

Library of Congress Card Catalogue No.: 94-75467
ISBN 1-56432-131-2

HUMAN RIGHTS WATCH

Human Rights Watch conducts regular, systematic investigations of human rights abuses in some seventy countries around the world. It addresses the human rights practices of governments of all political stripes, of all geopolitical alignments, and of all ethnic and religious persuasions. In internal wars it documents violations by both governments and rebel groups. Human Rights Watch defends freedom of thought and expression, due process and equal protection of the law; it documents and denounces murders, disappearances, torture, arbitrary imprisonment, exile, censorship and other abuses of internationally recognized human rights.

Human Rights Watch began in 1978 with the founding of its Helsinki division. Today, it includes five divisions covering Africa, the Americas, Asia, the Middle East, as well as the signatories of the Helsinki accords. It also includes four collaborative projects on arms, free expression, prison conditions, and women's rights. It maintains offices in New York, Washington, Los Angeles, London, Moscow, Belgrade, Zagreb and Hong Kong. Human Rights Watch is an independent, nongovernmental organization, supported by contributions from private individuals and foundations. It accepts no government funds, directly or indirectly.

The staff includes Kenneth Roth, executive director; Cynthia Brown, program director; Holly J. Burkhalter, advocacy director; Allyson Collins, research associate; Richard Dicker, associate counsel; Jamie Fellner, planning coordinator; Ham Fish, senior advisor; Barbara Guglielmo, comptroller; Robert Kimzey, publications director; Gara LaMarche, associate director; Michal Longfelder, development director; Ellen Lutz, California director; Juan Méndez, general counsel; Susan Osnos, communications director; Dinah PoKempner, research associate; Jemera Rone, counsel; Rachel Weintraub, special events director; and Derrick Wong, finance and administration director.

The regional directors of Human Rights Watch are Abdullahi An-Na'im, Africa; Juan E. Méndez, Americas; Sidney Jones, Asia; Jeri Laber, Helsinki; and Andrew Whitley, Middle East. The project directors are Kenneth Anderson, Arms Project; Gara LaMarche, Free Expression Project; Joanna Weschler, Prison Project; and Dorothy Q. Thomas, Women's Rights Project.

The board includes Robert L. Bernstein, chair; Adrian W. DeWind, vice chair; Roland Algrant, Lisa Anderson, Peter D. Bell, Alice L. Brown, William Carmichael, Dorothy Cullman, Irene Diamond, Jonathan Fanton, Alan Finberg, Jack Greenberg, Alice H. Henkin, Stephen L. Kass, Marina Pinto Kaufman, Alexander MacGregor, Peter Osnos, Kathleen Peratis, Bruce Rabb, Orville Schell, Gary G. Sick, and Malcolm Smith.

Addresses for Human Rights Watch

485 Fifth Avenue
New York, NY 10017-6104
Tel: (212) 972-8400
Fax: (212) 972-0905
email: hrwatchnyc@igc.apc.org

1522 K Street, N.W., #910
Washington, DC 20005
Tel: (202) 371-6592
Fax: (202) 371-0124
email: hrwatchdc@igc.apc.org

10951 West Pico Blvd., #203
Los Angeles, CA 90064
Tel: (310) 475-3070
Fax: (310) 475-5613
email: hrwatchla@igc.apc.org

90 Borough High Street
London, UK SE1 1LL
Tel: (071) 378-8008
Fax: (071) 378-8029
email: hrwatchuk@gn.apc.org

CONTENTS

ACKNOWLEDGMENTS

Research for this report was undertaken by Human Rights Watch/Helsinki researchers during September 1993-January 1994. The report was written by Julie Mertus, Counsel to Human Rights Watch/Helsinki and Vlatka Mihelić, a consultant to Human Rights Watch/Helsinki. It was edited by Jeri Laber, executive director of Human Rights Watch/Helsinki. Ivan Lupis and Christina Derry, Human Rights Watch/Helsinki associates, provided editorial assistance.

Human Rights Watch/Helsinki expresses its appreciation to the Open Society Fund for its invaluable support of its program in the former Yugoslavia, and to Genc Buçinca for his invaluable support and assistance in Kosovo.

INTRODUCTION AND SUMMARY OF CONCLUSIONS

With the world's attention focused on Bosnia-Hercegovina, Serbia apparently feels free to accelerate with impunity its violations of human rights in Kosovo. Police brutality and abuse in detention has long been "business as usual" in this province of Serbia, where Albanians comprise ninety percent of the population. Yet in 1993 the nature and scope of the abuse expanded markedly. Police raids on homes and marketplaces occur daily, and Serbian authorities have stepped up a campaign to push Albanians out of Serbian-populated areas. Heavily armed Serbian police and regular army forces patrol the streets in Kosovo, creating a state of terror. Increasingly, civilians report that regular army troops are involved in the shootings and harassment, acting alone or in concert with paramilitary forces. As of this writing, dozens of Albanians sit in jail, charged with terrorism and conspiracy to overthrow Yugoslavia. In a society run by brute force and intimidation, where the rule of law has completely disintegrated, it is unlikely that any of these men and women will see a fair trial.

By publishing the words of those who have been beaten and tortured by police — stories that have not been reported by any western press — this report seeks to demonstrate the prevalence and extreme brutality of police violence in Kosovo. The international community must listen and respond to these stories if long-term peace is ever to return to this troubled land. Few people in Kosovo (apart, perhaps, from Serb paramilitary groups) want an all-out war. For the Albanians of Kosovo, a war would be suicidal. The Serbian military and police contingents in Kosovo could quickly crush what appears to be a largely disarmed Albanian civilian population. Whether or not armed conflict erupts in Kosovo, gross human rights violations will continue unless the international community takes immediate action.

International human rights groups have had an increasingly difficult time working in Kosovo.[1] In 1993, Serb officials flatly rejected

---

[1] "Kosova" is the Albanian language term for "Kosovo." For the purposes of clarity, unless referring to a specific Albanian organization that includes "Kosova" in its name, this report uses "Kosovo" throughout. The report, however, provides the names of cities and villages in both Serbian and Albanian the first time the name is mentioned; at each additional reference, the official (Serbian) name is

the efforts of the Special Rapporteur for the United Nations Human Rights Commission to establish an office in Yugoslavia.[2] In July 1993, Yugoslavia kicked out the long-term Conference on Security and Cooperation in Europe (CSCE) monitoring mission from Kosovo and elsewhere, and then denied visas to United Nations personnel and to Amnesty International after they indicated a desire to visit Kosovo. In November 1993, police in Kosovo detained and interrogated a Human Rights Watch/Helsinki researcher who was preparing material for this report. Serb officials use intimidation and obstructionist tactics to prevent visitors from seeing what is happening in Kosovo.

Kosovo is a police state. Stripped of the relative autonomy it enjoyed in Tito's time, Kosovo is now under the direct and immediate control of Serb authorities who rule with an iron fist. Contesting the legitimacy of the 1990 constitutional amendments that rendered Kosovo subservient to Serbia, the Kosovo Albanians[3] have refused to sign oaths of loyalty to Serbia and Yugoslavia, and instead have organized defiantly for an independent Republic of Kosova.[4] Under constant government

---

used.

[2] "Yugoslavia" refers to the self-proclaimed Federal Republic of Yugoslavia, the union of Serbia (including the provinces of Vojvodina and Kosovo) and Montenegro. Although claiming successor status to the Socialist Federal Republic of Yugoslavia, the Federal Republic of Yugoslavia has not been internationally recognized as a successor state. Still, the current Yugoslav state's declaration that it wishes be recognized as a successor state implies that it is willing to accede to international agreements to which the former Yugoslavia was a party. Therefore, for the purpose of this report, all international obligations assumed by the former Yugoslavia will be transferred to the current state, including the obligations set forth in international and regional agreements to which the former Yugoslavia was a party, particularly the International Covenant on Civil and Political Rights, the Helsinki Final Act and subsequent CSCE documents. For a general statement on the duties of successor states, see Section 208 of the *Restatement of the Foreign Relations of the United States* (American Law Institute 1986).

[3] Throughout this report "Albanians" refers to ethnic Albanians in Kosovo.

[4] For a more detailed historical account, see The International Helsinki Federation, *From Autonomy to Colonization: Human Rights in Kosovo 1989-1993*, November 1993; and Helsinki Watch, *Yugoslavia: Human Rights Abuses in Kosovo,*

pressure Albanians have organized their own "parallel" schools, health care, welfare system and government, headed by Ibrahim Rugova, the leader of the largest Albanian party, the Democratic League of Kosova (LDK — Lidhja Demokratike e Kosoves), who was elected president of Kosova during Albanian-held elections in May 1992.[5]

On the one hand, Serbian authorities tolerate the "parallel" and pro-Kosovo activities of Albanians, allowing even Albanian human rights organizations to exist. On the other hand, Serbian authorities keep a tight lid on Albanian aspirations for independence through a program of forced displacement, harassment, arrest, interrogation and torture. Among other developments:

- *Serbian police have stepped up detention and arrests of Albanians with former Yugoslav military experience and of Albanian intellectuals.* These arrests neatly serve two goals of Serbian authorities. First, by charging the former military officers with conspiring to overthrow Yugoslavia, police spread fear that Albanians are planning an armed revolution. Second, should an uprising occur, the arrests effectively immobilize exactly those Albanians with the specific knowledge and skills necessary for plotting an armed rebellion. As the interviews presented in this report demonstrate, Serb authorities attribute the rash of recent arrests to an increase in Albanian attacks against police officers. Yet, to the best of Human Rights Watch/Helsinki's knowledge, no one has been charged in connection with such incidents.

- *Those tortured or beaten by the police have little recourse in Kosovo as the rule of law is practically nonexistent.* In a state where the judiciary has been robbed of its independence, defendants are routinely convicted solely on "confessions" signed after prolonged torture. This report details some

---

October 1992.

[5] For a description of police harassment during the Albanian elections, see Helsinki Watch, *Yugoslavia: Human Rights Abuses in Kosovo*, October 1992, pg. 20-22.

of the major court cases brought against Albanians in the latter half of 1993. Each case illustrates how non-Serbs in Kosovo are denied basic due process rights — from the right to counsel, to the right to remain silent, to the right to be free from torture.

• *Yugoslav army forces and paramilitary troops harass Albanian civilians with increasing frequency.* In one case, detailed in this report, two Yugoslav soldiers opened fire on two young Albanians near the unmarked border with Macedonia, killing one man and seriously wounding the other. The soldiers fired without warning and continued shooting even after the men had fallen down. Paramilitary forces have also been parading throughout Kosovo, preaching hatred of Albanians to Serbian villagers and harassing anyone who stands in their way. Villagers report that paramilitary forces now sometimes work in conjunction with regular police.

• *The Serb-orchestrated forced displacement of Albanians has begun.* In the summer of 1993, in at least four villages near the thin strip of predominantly Serbian villages in northern Kosovo, heavily-armed police squadrons invaded houses, conducted unwarranted searches, and brutally beat and detained Albanians of all ages. While such raids have occurred in the past, the new campaign includes specific threats aimed at terrorizing villagers so they will leave their homes. Authorities in charge of deeds and land supplement the raids on border villages. In September 1993, the municipal authorities and regular police began demanding that Albanians present proof of ownership of their land. Inevitably, the authorities reject whatever deed the villagers produce and order them to vacate their property immediately.

Along with the escalation of police and military abuse of non-Serb civilians, the economic status of Albanians and other non-Serbs in Kosovo has declined. Many Albanian families subsist solely on contributions sent by relatives working abroad. Most Albanian children are schooled in private homes, and police routinely harass, detain, and interrogate them and their teachers for attending the "illegal" Albanian-run schools. Most Albanian doctors, having been laid off *en masse* two years ago, practice medicine in store front operations run on shoestring budgets, charging little or nothing for services. And a fledgling Albanian-run welfare system continues to aid a large percentage of the population, despite Serb interference with humanitarian aid sent from abroad.

The purpose of this report is not to offer a complete list of human rights violations — as, unfortunately, the magnitude of abuse renders that impossible — nor is it to repeat information published elsewhere.[6] Rather, by drawing from Human Rights Watch/Helsinki's own first hand interviews in Kosovo conducted in the latter half of 1993, this report seeks to describe some of the most recent and pressing developments.

Among other recommendations set forth in this report, Human Rights Watch/Helsinki calls on the government of Serbia to immediately:

- Cease the harassment, interrogation and arrest of individuals who meet with or aid foreign delegations;

- Cease the harassment, interrogation and arrest of local and foreign individuals and groups who investigate human rights abuses in Kosovo;

- Prosecute individuals, members of paramilitary groups and the police that harass political and ethnic minorities and carry guns illegally;

---

[6] For other accounts, see The International Helsinki Federation, *From Autonomy to Colonization: Human Rights in Kosovo 1989-1993*, November 1993; Helsinki Watch, *Human Rights Abuses in Kosovo*, October 1992; Michael W. Galligan et. al., "The Kosovo Crisis and Human Rights in Yugoslavia: A Report of the Committee on International Human Rights," Record of the Association of the Bar of the City of New York, Vol. 46, No. 3, April 1991; Helsinki Watch and International Helsinki Federation, *Yugoslavia: Crisis in Kosovo*, March 1990; Helsinki Watch, *Increasing Turbulence: Human Rights in Yugoslavia*, October 1989.

- Investigate Yugoslav army recruits and officers responsible for use of undue force against Albanian civilians;

- Cease all police, military and other activity aimed at forcibly removing non-Serbs from their homes;

- Immediately cease the use of torture against detainees;

- Investigate and punish police and security officers responsible for treating Albanians in detention in an inhumane manner;

- End random street stops and searches and require a warrant for entering a private residence or business;

- Allow persons to assemble freely at peaceful gatherings including meetings which are aimed at criticizing the Serbian government or Serbian rule;

- Respect the freedom of the press and the freedom of speech and expression of all persons and organizations in Kosovo;

- Reinstate an independent judiciary with respect for due process and the rule of law;

- Drop all charges against persons who have been indicted for peaceful expression of opinion or for membership in a group which is banned or looked upon unfavorably by the Serbian government;

- Drop all pending and future charges based solely on "confessions" extracted by force, as well as charges based solely on material discovered in searches without warrants;

- Cease the harassment, beatings and interrogations of Albanian educators and school children, and provide access to education on a nondiscriminatory basis;

- Reinstate all of those unlawfully dismissed from their jobs because of ethnic or political affiliation;

The international community must act as well. The United Nations and the CSCE should declare that Serbian officials' treatment of ethnic and political minorities in Yugoslavia, including Kosovo, is in violation of international human rights norms. At the same time, the United Nations and the CSCE should take immediate steps to reinstate long term human rights monitors in Kosovo. Given the detailed documentation of human rights abuses in the region, no justification exists for continued inaction.

POLICE VIOLENCE AND MISTREATMENT IN DETENTION

RECENT TRENDS

Police violence and mistreatment in detention has escalated since the CSCE human rights monitors left Kosovo in July 1993. One particularly significant development, detailed below, has been a new campaign of police raids against border towns in northern Kosovo, apparently designed to push Albanians out of Serbian populated areas. The prevalence and intensity of police terror in 1993 increased, with police attacking everyone from old men on the streets and in marketplaces for no reason whatsoever, to shootings of young men in their cars and homes for purported involvement in police killings and other Albanian "terrorist" activities.[1] According to the U.S. State Department, a total of fifteen Albanians died at the hands of police in 1993.[2]

The Council on Human Rights and Freedoms ("the Council"), the largest and most active Albanian human rights organization in Kosovo, reported over 5,700 incidents[3] of police abuse in 1992. According to the Council, the number of incidents of police abuse increased dramatically in 1993, with more than 5,700 cases of police maltreatment and 1,400

---

[1] According to the Kosovo Helsinki Committee and Human Rights Watch/Helsinki's own research, most beatings, shootings and other forms of harassment of Albanian civilians are committed by police and state security officers, not by the military. Human Rights Watch/Helsinki interview with Gazmend Pula, leader of the Kosova Helsinki Committee in Priština/Prishtinë, September 1993.

[2] U.S. Department of State, *Country Reports on Human Rights Practices for 1993*, (February 1994).

[3] Note that this number includes only "reported" incidents, that is cases in which the abused person, a witness, or a human rights researcher provided the details to the Council. Cases in which no witness is present and the abused person is too afraid to report the incident are not included.

1

arrests reported in the first eight months alone.[4] Ibrahim Rugova, the
head of the Albanian "parallel" government, similarly reported a sharp
increase in police abuse in the latter half of 1993, stating that from June
through September 1993, police raided over 2,500 homes.[5]

The Kosovo Secretary of Information, Boško Drobnjak, argued
that the number of Albanian attacks *against* police officers has also
increased, contending that "in the past year, [1992-1993] there have been
130 terrorist attacks on police." In his opinion, the attacks were
committed by Albanian "extremist groups, not by Mr. Rugova." Although
no one has been charged in the attacks, Mr. Drobnjak claims that police
have determined that the bullets used were produced in China and "it is
well known that Albanians have Chinese arms and ammunition, probably
delivered from Albania."[6]

Human Rights Watch/Helsinki has not received any evidence of
Albanian attacks against the police and, according to Serbian authorities
in the fall of 1993, no one has been charged for the purported crimes.
At the same time, while Human Rights Watch/Helsinki is unable to
confirm each and every case of police abuse reported by the Council and
other local human rights groups, its own independent research confirms
that police terror against Albanian civilians is on the rise.

SPECIFIC CASES

Specific incidents of abuse, illustrating six types of abuse, are
detailed below.

Police Raids on Villages

Serbian police have long raided Albanian villages under the
pretext of weapon searches. This section highlights a variant of this
problem: organized attempts to push Albanians out of Serbian-populated
areas. Although these raids are less prevalent than weapon searches, they

---

[4] Human Rights Watch/Helsinki interview in Priština, September 1993.

[5] Human Rights Watch/Helsinki interview in Priština, October 1993.

[6] Human Rights Watch/Helsinki interview in Priština, September 1993.

represent a comparatively new phenomenon that intensified in scope over 1993.

Reports indicate that Serbian police, joined on occasion by paramilitary squads, have begun a campaign of violence against Albanian-inhabited villages situated near the predominantly Serbian town of Leposavić/Leposaviq.[7] Although police have raided Albanian villages in this area before, the new campaign is accompanied by specific threats designed to push Albanians out of this thin strip of Serbian populated land. As such, these raids seem to represent a new phenomena.

Čabra/Çabër: An Example of Police Terror in Border Villages

Villagers in Čabra, an impoverished village on Kosovo's border with Serbia proper and Montenegro, have long been terrorized by regular police officers, paramilitary troops, and armed Serbian civilians. As one man testified, "Here we feel like rabbits. The Serbs stand on the edge of the road and take shots at us and we have nowhere to go."[8] The harassment intensified in 1993, as villagers began sighting police and paramilitary troops with increasing frequency. The number of villagers picked up by police and taken to the station for questioning also escalated during this period.

One man, S.H., reported that twice in June the police called him into the station for interrogation sessions. Each time, they asked him whether he or any other villagers had weapons.

The first time they kept me for five hours. The second for six hours. They didn't beat me, but they insulted me as an Albanian and as a member of the LDK. They also threatened that if I didn't leave my place, they would kill me. They tried to make me work for them, to be a spy.

---

[7] The town of Leposavić has a Serbian majority. The overall municipality is predominately Albanian.

[8] Human Rights Watch/Helsinki interview in Čabra, September 1993.

> "You will be well paid and we will give you a gun," they
> promised.[9]

Other villagers stated that police had made similar promises to them in
exchange for spying on their neighbors. All vehemently insisted that they
refused the offers.

The events in Čabra came to a head when the police launched a
full scale raid on the village. On August 26, 1993, about 200 police
surrounded the area, searched 130 Albanian homes, made seven arrests
and beat approximately seventy people.[10]

The villagers had suspected that something was going to happen
because they spotted police officers casing the area few days before the
incident. To prepare for whatever could happen, villagers took turns
watching over the village throughout the night. Musa Rama, one of the
men who had been on the lookout, explained what he saw.

> I was in the woods, above the village with four others
> when, at about 5:15 A.M., we saw a large number of
> police in uniforms coming toward the village, maybe 250
> - 300 of them. When I saw them, I started to run
> because I was afraid since I'm on the list for mobilization
> for the army. I hid with the others. ... During the time
> that I was hiding there, I heard the voices of people who
> were being beaten.[11]

The view from the village was one of terror, as S.H. similarly
remembered:

> I heard the noises of police cars and when I looked out
> the window, I saw that my house was surrounded by

---

[9] Human Rights Watch/Helsinki interview in Čabra, September 1993. Name
withheld to protect witness.

[10] These numbers were given to Human Rights Watch/Helsinki by the
villagers of Čabra. The figures listed by the LDK of Mitrovica/Mitrovicë state that
the police raided 140 houses, beat fifty three people and made six arrests.

[11] Human Rights Watch/Helsinki interview in Čabra, September 1993.

police. They broke down my door to get inside. They
demanded, "Who is the owner of this house?" I told
them that I was. They told me to come with them
upstairs, and they told the rest of my family to go
outside. Four of the policemen started to beat me with
their machine guns, sticks, fists, whatever they could.
[He showed a scar on his calf, below his knee.][12]

One eighty-year-old woman, Grisha Kamberi, reportedly suffered
a stroke during the raid. Police burst into her home and began beating
all of her adult family members, men first and then women. She
collapsed and, according to the LDK Human Rights Commission, died
four days later.

Police raided Sherif Rama's house as well, as she testified:

They came inside the house without asking and started
to search. They found an old shotgun and said, "What is
this?" I said "It is an old shotgun that belonged to my
father-in-law and it is very old and we have documents
for it." I told them that there were only women in this
house. The police started to shout and say, "You must
leave this country and go to Albania where you
belong."[13]

At the same time, another group of police raided Zaim Deliu's
house in a similar manner:

About 5:15 in the morning, about seven or eight police
officers came to my house, broke down the door and
went inside. They gathered my whole family in front of
the house, my eight children, my ninety-eight-year-old
father and my wife. After an hour or so, another group
of policemen, about twelve or thirteen of them, came and

---

[12] Human Rights Watch/Helsinki interview in Čabra, September 1993.

[13] Human Rights Watch/Helsinki interview in Čabra, September 1993.

they started to search the house and they were asking,
"Where are your weapons?"[14]

While the police searched the house, the family waited outside in their
night clothes. Mr. Deliu continued:

> At about 7:15 A.M., three police came to the house and
> called me by name, telling me to come inside. As soon
> as I went inside, one of them hit me in the face and said,
> "Tell me where is your gun. You will tell us where the
> others keep their weapons, or we shall kill you." I told
> them, "I don't have any weapons and I don't know where
> there are any weapons in this village." That moment, the
> same policeman hit me in the stomach with his fist while
> two others grabbed my hands and held them. After that,
> they started to ask me the same questions, and I
> continued to give them the same answers. One of them
> kicked me in the ribs and I felt a terrible pain. (Later,
> when I went to the doctor, he said that my 11th rib was
> broken.)
>
> After that, one of them tried to hit me with a machine
> gun in the head, but I put my arm up to block it, and he
> struck me in the wrist. The policeman told me that he
> would kill me unless I talked. When I refused, he held
> the machine gun above his head, and then brought it
> down as if he was going to hit me, stopping only one to
> two centimeters from my head. After that, the police
> continued to beat me. They smacked me in the mouth
> with their fists and I started bleeding. One of them gave
> me a handkerchief and told me to clean up the blood.
> They said, "We don't want the others to see you
> bleeding."[15]

---

[14] Human Rights Watch/Helsinki interview in Čabra, September 1993.

[15] Human Rights Watch/Helsinki interview in Čabra, September 1993.

While some police searched houses in this manner, others trampled the woods surrounding the village looking for new victims. A group of about twenty officers eventually found the group hiding in the woods. Mr. Rama recalled what happened next:

> When the police found us, they started to beat us. They beat us with their boots and the butts of machine guns. The police said to us, "Where are your weapons? Where are the bunkers where you keep the weapons?" They said, "Tell us, it is better to tell us, we know there are weapons because your neighbors told us."[16]

Mr. Rama and many others said that the police frequently claim that they have information from their neighbors in order to cause dissention.

For twenty men, the abuse did not end after the police left their homes. Rather, the beatings continued after police brought them to the central location that was serving as the headquarters for the police operation. Mr. Rama was one of these men:

> After they beat us, they gathered us with about twenty others they had caught. They put us in handcuffs and told us that we must leave this country within three months. "It is not your place here," they said, "Leave or we will kill you."

Another one of the men who was gathered with the group of twenty, Aziz Hasani, testified as to particularly brutal treatment:

> About eight officers came to my house to beat me. I recognized some of the police from around town and knew at least one of them by name. They kicked me until I fell down from the blows. Two of them pinned me down with their legs and they started to ask, "Where are your bunkers, your hiding places for weapons?" During the time I was on the ground, they continued to beat me. They kicked me in the mouth with their boots

---

[16] Human Rights Watch/Helsinki interview in Čabra, September 1993.

and kicked me in the left ear. I still don't hear well in
that ear. I am very embarrassed because they beat me
like that in front of my wife and children.[17]

After police finished beating him, Mr. Hasani said they brought
him to the same central place where they had brought all of the other
men.

When I arrived with the others, they said, "You must go
to Albania. If we come back and find you here, we will
kill you all.   If you stay here, you must forget the
Albanian language, all that is Albanian. You will learn
the Serbian language and you will talk to each other in
the Serbian language. ... I answered, "We were born here
and we will die here and we will never leave this
country."

They asked me to which party I belonged. I answered
that I belonged to the party of Ibrahim Rugova. They
then said, "Look here, we just beat you up, but when
Šešelj's police come, they will kill you all. Why don't you
rise up and start the war?" I said, "We don't want a war
here, we want to get what we want in a peaceful way."

At about 10:15 A.M., the police left the village for the police
station.   They took only four of the men from the temporary
headquarters with them, Aziz Hasani, Sherif Rama, Sadri Hasani and
Shemsi Jakupi. According to Mr. Hasani, the police beat him during the
entire ride to the police station. Although the police did not beat them
at the station, they did question the men some more.   Mr. Hasani
testified:

They made a file on me. They kept me there for about
six hours. Before they released me, they took my ID.

---

[17] Human Rights Watch/Helsinki interview in Čabra, September 1993. At the
time of the interview with Human Rights Watch/Helsinki, Mr. Hasani still had
scars from the beatings.

> This means that I'm now confined in this village. It is
> too dangerous to go outside it without an ID.

A doctor later diagnosed Mr. Hasani with two broken ribs, large
hematomas, and injury to his left ear that impaired his hearing.

The villagers now fear that the police will seize the land that they
legally own and force them to move. According to many villagers, since
the August raid the police have returned nearly daily. Villagers speculate
that "police are making some maps." Villagers are terrified about what
could happen. As one man worried, "We are threatened by physical
liquidation. I worry that they are trying to force us to begin a war."[18]

Deeds checks

Around the 13th or 14th of September 1993, the municipal
authorities asked one of the men they had beaten during the August raid
in Čabra to produce the deeds to his land, which is located near a
Serbian-populated area.

> I have good documents for the land. When I brought
> them to the authorities they looked at them and said,
> "You cannot use your land." They said that the deed was
> too old. They wanted a deed from 1961, not the one
> that I had from 1951.[19]

Villagers in Čabra knew of eighteen families who had been
ordered to produce the deeds to their land. In no case did the Serbian
authorities accept the deed that was presented. According to one man,
after the authorities rejected his deed, he went to his land and some
Serbian civilians were there waiting for him, ready to kill him. They shot
seven times in his direction, he claimed, but he escaped by fleeing into
the woods.

The police began using this new tack on the villagers in northern
Kosovo in mid-August, when they first required some villagers to prove
ownership of their homes and land. On August 15, the municipal

---

[18] Human Rights Watch/Helsinki interview in Čabra, September 1993.

[19] Human Rights Watch/Helsinki interview in Čabra, September 1993.

authorities and regular police went into villages in this area and asked for eighteen families to produce their deeds. They told them to bring all of their documents to a nearby town. According to the local LDK leader:

> The families brought documents dating to 1951. When the authorities saw that, they said that they needed more recent documents. When the villagers brought documents from 1961, the authorities rejected them and said "We will build strategic things for the state on the land where your house sits."[20]

Villagers from areas north of Priština/Prishtinë independently have reported similar accounts.[21]

The Flight of Albanians From Border Villages

• **Bistrica/Bistricë**

A subset of the village of Bistrica, a gathering of five houses about twenty minutes walk from the center of Bistrica, was one of the first to be raided by the police. On March 11, 1992, an estimated 200 police officers descended upon the houses in a great display of force. Xhafer Hajdari explained:

> At 7 A.M., police forces came and surrounded our five houses. There were about 200 to 250 of them. Seven of them went inside my house, shouting as loud as they could. I got in front of them and said, "Don't shout. This is my house. I am the host of this house. I built it myself." The police only shouted more. ... They began hitting me, on the back of my head, chest, hands. Six of them hit me. One of them held a machine gun, which he pointed at my family. ... They started asking me, "Who is supporting you?" [He had been fired from his job.] "Does Rugova support you?" Then they told me that I

---

[20] Human Rights Watch/Helsinki interview in Mitrovica, September 1993.

[21] Accounts gathered by Human Rights Watch/Helsinki representatives in Mitrovica, September 1993.

must leave this place and go to Albania. They threatened
that if I didn't go, they would kill me.[22]

Mr. Hajdari testified that three of the men who raided his house
were civilians wearing bulletproof vests and carrying machine guns. He
recognized some of them by name. The officers raided the houses,
ostensibly looking for weapons. Mrs. Hajdari testified as well:

> One of them put a machine gun to my neck and said,
> "Tell me, tell me, where are your weapons, or I'll kill
> your children!" I showed them one hunting rifle that we
> had legal permission to own and they took it.

Police took Mr. Hajdari and his seventeen-year-old son to the
police station where they confined them in separate rooms for
interrogations and beatings. Mr. Hajdari remembered:

> During all of that time, they beat me. And they keep
> saying "Who is supporting you? Why don't you work?"
> ... A police officer put my hand on the floor and another
> stomped on it. They smashed me in the side and broke
> two of my ribs. One of them hit me in the back of my
> head with something — I don't know what — and I lost
> consciousness. When I woke up, my head was wet with
> water. They were trying to get me to wake up. My face
> was all bloody and I had lost teeth. They warned me
> that I must go to Albania or else.

Mr. Hajdari's teenage son was also badly beaten. Since that time, he has
been unable to go to school.
    Two weeks after the assault, all five families living in the isolated
hamlet decided to leave their homes. Mr. Hajdari explained:

> We were very afraid. Three weeks before the raid, we
> had noticed some armed men in strange uniforms. From
> the looks of their uniforms, which were grey swirls like

---

[22] Human Rights Watch/Helsinki interview in Mitrovica, September 1993.

camouflage, we presumed [that they were] Šešelj's troops.
They were walking around our houses with their
weapons. This made us decide to leave as well.

All of the families are now living temporarily in cramped quarters of
houses donated by other Albanians in Mitrovica/Mitrovicë. A similar
scenario occurred in Koštovo — another village in northern Kosovo - with
many villagers also fleeing to Mitrovica.[23]

• Ceraja/Cerajë
        Fearful that the police raids on Bistrica and Koštovo would be
repeated again in their own village, eight Albanian families from Ceraja,
a village of thirty two houses approximately three kilometers from
Bistrica and Koštovo, fled to Mitrovica. The patriarch of one of these
families gave their story:

> We were terrorized by our Serbian neighbors, police and
> army. For example, when we had to travel by bus, the
> buses would be filled with soldiers and they would offend
> us with ethnic slurs, call us offending names, and
> threaten us. ...

> The first visit by police forces was in April 1992. They
> surrounded the village and they announced that they had
> a list of seven or eight "rag roots" — young men that
> must go into the Yugoslav army. That day, they raided
> six houses. They didn't beat anyone; they just gave
> fathers an ultimatum that they must bring their sons
> within twenty four hours to the police station so that they
> could be sent into the Yugoslav army. Of course, they
> never went to the police station.

> In July 1993, we saw many police again near the village.
> Some were on foot; some in cars. A few days after that,
> we learned of the police raids in Bistrica and Koštovo.
> After that we were very frightened. We were so

_____

[23] Accounts gathered by Human Rights Watch/Helsinki representatives in
Mitrovica, September 1993.

frightened that we left our houses and our land where we
had lived for many centuries. We were afraid that the
same fate would happen to us.[24]

One of the other men who fled had been an eyewitness to the
police raids on Koštovo and Bistrica. He remembered:

I was married that day, and when I was coming home,
crossing near the village, I saw many, many police and I
heard a lot of people screaming. I went back home and
told others what happened. We decided to leave as soon
as we could.[25]

A total of eight families, approximately seventy five people, fled
Ceraja for Mitrovica.[26]   Most of them live in homes vacated by
Albanians who have fled the country, or in cramped quarters doubled up
with relatives.

Other Police Raids on Villages

Random raids on villages throughout Kosovo under the pretext
of weapon searches present a much more prevalent problem than the
border raids. Each village is at risk, not just those close to the border.
During such raids, police, at times reportedly aided by armed civilians
and/or paramilitary troops, indiscriminately beat villagers regardless of
their sex or age.

For example, villagers from Gornje Nerodimlje/Nerodime e
Epërme (near Uroševac/Ferizaj) report that on September 15, 1993, at
about 5:30 A.M., about 200 policemen, traveling on foot and in about
twenty police cars and three armed personnel carriers (APCs), surrounded
part of their village. They raided homes, searching residents for
weapons. Women police reportedly searched women residents while

[24] Human Rights Watch/Helsinki interview in Mitrovica, September 1993.

[25] Human Rights Watch/Helsinki interview in Mitrovica, September 1993.

[26] Human Rights Watch/Helsinki spoke with two of these families in
Mitrovica, September 1993.

male police searched and beat the male residents.   One resident
explained:

> The police raided all of our houses looking for who
> knows what. They found an Albanian flag and burnt it
> and a photo of Rugova and threatened to kill the man
> that had the photo. All of this lasted about three hours.
> In total, they raided about fifteen houses. Then they
> marched through the village.   No one was arrested.
> They just wanted to frighten us.[27]

Residents in Gnjilane/Gjilan similarly report that immediately
after the CSCE mission left Kosovo, police raided twenty homes,
ostensibly in searches for weapons.   According to an LDK leader in
Gnjilane, police have tried a new tack in connection with such raids:
Police coerce Albanians to buy weapons and then immediately search
them for the weapons and arrest them.[28] Human Rights Watch/Helsinki
received reports of similar raids on dozens of villages in the summer and
fall of 1993.

Civilians Shot Dead By Police

Summary of Incidents Since CSCE Withdrawal

Shootings of Albanian civilians usually occur in connection with
a border incident or with the type of raids on houses described above,
with the police justifying the assault by claiming that the fleeing Albanian
was armed and dangerous. Since the CSCE withdrawal, human rights
activists in Kosovo report an increase in such incidents over the previous
year. Although Human Rights Watch/Helsinki has not been able to
confirm independently any precise figures on the number of Albanian
civilians shot by police or border guards in the summer and fall of 1993,
its research indicates that indeed police have used unjustified gun fire
against unarmed Albanian civilians. One such case is documented below.

---

[27] Human Rights Watch/Helsinki interview in Uroševac, October 1993. Name
withheld to protect witness.

[28] Human Rights Watch/Helsinki interview in Gnjilane, October 1993.

Death of a Boy in Uroševac

On August 25, 1993, police shot and killed sixteen-year-old year-old Sefer Qukovci in Cernila/Cërrnillë, an Albanian village in the vicinity of Uroševac. Sefer's uncle, Enver, recounted what happened:

> At 5:00 A.M. in the morning on August 25, the police surrounded Sefer's house. ... They searched the house and harassed Sefer's mother, Remzija. They were looking for her older sons, twenty-six-year-old Kadri and twenty-eight-year-old Fatmir. But none of her sons were at home, and she told the police that she didn't know where they were. The police told her to report to the police station in Babuše/Babush at noon that day.[29]

The brothers returned home at 9:00 A.M.. The policemen had never left, Enver recalled, they had simply hid in the yard waiting for the young men:

> The brothers were in the yard with other family members when the shooting began. ... Three policemen shot from about 100 meters away. The brothers tried to flee. They ran across the yard and into a cornfield. The police ran after them.

Sefer's mother saw Dragiša Spasić, a local Serbian policeman, aim and shoot at her youngest son, Sefer. After he fell, screaming in pain, police restrained his mother from running to him. According to Enver:

> The police didn't let anyone near his body. After they shot him, more policemen arrived. There were about sixty of them. They surrounded the house and no one was allowed in or out. At about 4:00 P.M., the police took his body away. We don't know where they took him.

---

[29] Human Rights Watch/Helsinki interview in Uroševac, October 1993.

The next day, the family retrieved Sefer's body from the hospital in Priština. A week later, the police came again for the older brothers, Kadri and Fatmir, but they had already fled. While the police never clearly stated why they wanted the brothers, their family believes that it is because Fatmir deserted from the army and Kadri refused even to go.

Police then harassed the imam who presided over the young man's funeral. On August 26, the imam, Hamdi Cerkini, traveled to the village of Cernila for the funeral ceremony. According to the imam, who washed Sefer's body to prepare him for burial, the boy had been shot three times in the back.[30] The imam remembered being observed during the ceremony:

> We noticed a few men in a white car that was about a
> half kilometer away from us. They were watching us
> with binoculars. When the funeral was finished, we
> started to go back. We were in a place called Babush —
> me and two colleagues — when we were stopped by the
> men in the white car.[31]

The men in the white car forced the driver to park on the side of the road. As is standard practice in Kosovo, the police offered no reason for stopping them, and gave no reason for asking for identification.

> While one of the policemen told the driver to give his ID,
> another policeman told my colleague and me to step
> outside. The police took the man in the passenger seat
> five or six meters from the car, and he shouted to me,
> "Come here quickly." When I arrived there, he said,
> "Give me your ID." When I reached into my pocket to
> get my ID, he suddenly hit me in the face with the heel
> of his hand. He smacked me about four times. He asked
> me what I told the people at the funeral. He called me

---

[30] The imam who presided over the young man's funeral on August 26, 1993, testified as to the condition of the body: "I could see that there were three shots, one in the shoulder and two in the chest. The body was bloody from being dragged." Human Rights Watch/Helsinki interview in Uroševac, October 1993.

[31] Human Rights Watch/Helsinki interview in Uroševac, October 1993.

a nationalist and a separatist and said that I had made
propaganda against the state.

I moved away from the policeman. I was spitting blood.
When I tried to speak, the other policeman came up
behind me and said, "Are you trying to escape?" And he
hit me with a club across my back. The first one who hit
me then hit me again, in the face about three times with
his fists.

According to the imam, the police beat the driver of his car as
well. At this point, the imam testified, about four or five additional
policeman joined them.

One of these officers tried to stop them from beating us.
He said "Enough! What are you doing?" ... The
policeman who had hit me so any times warned me, "If
you held a speech at the funeral, God himself can't save
you." I told them that I didn't go there to give a speech
but just to do my job.

After the police quizzed the men about the funeral, they eventually gave
back their identification and let them leave.

Torture and Death in Detention

Summary of Recent Incidents

Human Rights Watch/Helsinki has collected scores of testimony
on mistreatment in prison and other forms of police detention. The
abuse ranges from verbal abuse to severe beatings on all parts of the
body, including genitals and the soles of the feet — with truncheons, rifle
butts, fists or boots. According to the Kosovo Helsinki Committee, since
August 23, 1993, at least two persons have died as a result of
mistreatment while in police custody.[32] In February 1993, Adem Seqiri
from Ðakovica/Gjakova was arrested and beaten to death in the police

---

[32] Human Rights Watch/Helsinki interview in Priština, September 1993.

station. In August, Arif Krasniqi died at the hands of police in Prizren.
Human Rights Watch/Helsinki has investigated the latter incident, as
recounted below. The second case below details but one example of the
type of abuse police inflict on Albanians in detention. For a discussion of
the attempts of defense lawyers to report such abuse, see below.

Murder of Arif Krasniqi in the Prizren Police Station

On August 30, 1993, Arif Krasniqi, a forty-two-year-old father of
eight from Atmagja (a village near Prizren), was carried out of the police
station in Prizren dead.   Under the pretext that Krasniqi owned a
handgun without a proper license, two policemen — Momir Jašović and
Tihomir Kosović — had arrested him in a street in Prizren that evening
at about 5:15 P.M. The police officers had found no weapons when they
searched Mr. Krasniqi's truck. Still, they took him to the Prizren police
station and used excessive force during the interrogation. As a result of
torture, Mr. Krasniqi died in the police station an hour after his arrival.

Mr. Selajdin Braha, a fifty-five-year-old Albanian, was detained
in the same police station. Mr. Braha witnessed the abuse:

> On the 30th of August I was in the prison yard with
> other prisoners for our daily walk. From where I was in
> the yard, I had a good view of the state security offices.
> They had opened the windows. I didn't know who the
> man was, but I could hear blows, and I heard the
> policemen saying, "You have weapons," and him
> answering, "I don't have weapons." This went back and
> forth again and again. The man said, "No, I swear by
> my children," and then he repeated it several times. And
> then he said, "I don't have it. I'll spend 10,000 deutsche
> marks to buy it." I was walking around the yard all this
> time. This was very hard to hear because I could tell
> that the outcome would be tragic.
>
> When I got back into my cell, I could still see what was
> happening. The windows of the state security building
> are lower than the windows of the prison and they are
> right across from each other so everyone can see in when
> they open the windows. I could see that two policemen

kept going in and out of the room. We all heard the screams and then eventually it became silent. The next day, we heard that the man had been killed. The policemen who killed him were put in our same prison the next day. Even the government admitted that they had gone too far.[33]

Dr. Slaviša Dobričanin of the Institute for Forensic Medicine in Priština performed the autopsy on August 31 at the request of the President of the Prizren District Court, Nikola Vazura. According to the autopsy report, Mr. Krasniqi had multiple bruises and wounds over his entire body. He also suffered numerous internal injuries, including broken bones that damaged his vital organs. Dr. Dobričanin concluded: "[Arif Krasniqi's] death was violent and is due to a shock. This shock is a result of the numerous wounds and subcutaneous bleeding. The wounds were inflicted with great force by a heavy, blunt object."[34]

On September 1, 1993, authorities detained Mr. Jašović and Mr. Kosović, the two police officers who had beaten Mr. Krasniqi to death. District Public Prosecutor Dobrivoje Perić indicted them on October 6, under Article 53 of the Criminal Code of the Republic of Serbia,[35]

---

[33] Human Rights Watch/Helsinki interview in a village near Prizren, October 1993.

[34] *Autopsy Report number 126/93*, Priština University Medical School, Institute for Forensic Medicine, dated August 31, 1993.

[35] Article 53 of the Criminal Code of Serbia provides that:
(1) Someone who inflicts another with a serious injury or permanently damages another person's health will be sentenced to between six months and five years in prison.
(2) Someone who causes another such injury or damages his health to the extent that this person's life is jeopardized, or some vital organ is destroyed or permanently disabled, or if the other person is disabled for life, or if his health is permanently damaged, or if he is disfigured, will be sentenced to between one and ten years in prison.
(3) If the other person dies as a result of injuries specified in Paragraphs 1 and 2 of this Article, the perpetrator will be sentenced to between one and twelve years in prison.
(...)

charging them with "physically hurting Arif Krasniqi by inflicting him
with a series of injuries and causing him subcutaneous bleeding resulting
in a state of shock that led to Krasniqi's death.[36]

The indictment cites the statement of another policeman,
Bogoljub Prodanović, attesting that he was present for five to ten minutes
"in office number 6 while the accused, using force, inflicted several blows
to Krasniqi over the palms of his hands and the soles of his feet." In
direct contradiction, other witnesses claim that Mr. Prodanović himself,
along with Ramo Oruči and a driver by the name of Djuka, joined in
beating Mr. Krasniqi. In spite of the lawyers' requests, neither of these
three men were called to testify.

Fellow policemen warmly greeted Jašović and Kosović as they
arrived in the courtroom for the trial on November 23, 1993 and
threatened the Krasniqi family's lawyers. After a short trial, the court
found Mr. Jašović and Mr. Kosović guilty and sentenced them both to
three years in prison, but immediately released them pending their
appeal.

Torture of LDK Leader in Uroševac

A number of LDK activists from Uroševac were arrested in the
spring and summer of 1993 under allegations that they had been storing
arms and planning Albanian supremacist activities. One of them, Ismet
Hasani, a thirty-eight-year-old activist from Uroševac, was arrested on
May 20, 1993, and kept in custody for four months. His case, although
far from unique, serves to illustrate the kind of torture Serbian police
inflict on Albanian prisoners. Less than two weeks after he was finally
released, in mid-September 1993, he spoke with Human Rights
Watch/Helsinki about his ordeal:

> On May 20, 1993, at 10:30 P.M., I was in my home with
> my wife and two friends. The police — four uniformed
> officers and two plain clothes inspectors — came looking
> for me. One of them I knew by name, Srečko. I later
> noticed that many more policemen were in the front
> yard. They searched the house for weapons although I

---

[36] *Indictment of Momir Jašović and Tihomir Kosović,* filed in Prizren on October
6, 1993.

told them that I had none. Four policemen beat me in front of my children while the inspector held a machine gun pointed at me. They slapped me and hit me with clubs for about fifteen or twenty minutes. I had nothing to confess.[37]

After beating him in his house, the policemen put him in a car and took him to the Uroševac police station.

[At the station,] they beat me again, insisting that I admit to smuggling guns. I told them that I don't smuggle guns. They beat me again, demanding that I tell them where I hid the guns. But I had no guns to hide!

They beat me all night. I could not lift my head to see how many people were hitting me with clubs and fists. They kicked me. I insisted that they show me the person who claims that I gave him the gun, but they refused. Eventually, they brought in the LDK secretary [who had been arrested earlier][38] and said that I gave him guns. He said that I offered him nothing. They beat us both again.

This time, Mr. Hasani testified, the torture began in full force.

Another inspector, wearing a sweatsuit and sneakers came to the room and said that I should confess since they do not like to beat people. I thought that he was nicer than the rest and I asked for a cigarette. At that, he turned around and kicked me so hard in the chest that I flew over to the other side of the room. I could not get up. With me still on the ground, they pried my shoes off. One of them held my head against the wall while the other four beat me on my feet. They then hit

---

[37] Human Rights Watch/Helsinki interview in Uroševac, October 1993.

[38] The authorities released the LDK secretary the next day.

me repeatedly across my back with clubs. I was sure I
was dying.

They put my feet and hands in a bucket of cold water
and two policemen continued to hit me with clubs on my
ears. They told me to lift my arm when I was ready to
confess.

Mr. Hasani, however, did not confess, and his torturers eventually
gave up for the evening, dragging Mr. Hasani off to spend the night in
a basement cell. The next morning, the torture began again.

I still refused to sign a confession, so they took me to a
gym where one man boxed me for about ten minutes.
He said that I was lucky that he had hurt his hand
beating someone else, otherwise I would not have it so
easy.

They left me alone for a while and four other policemen
came. They tied my feet together and made me lie on
my stomach with my arms stretched out. They stepped
on my fingers and beat me on the feet and kidneys.

Eventually, the policemen took Mr. Hasani back to Srečko, the
inspector who had arrested him.

Srečko said that there was no need to beat me anymore.
At that, Srečko picked up a machine gun and pointed it
at my head and said, "Confess or I will shoot you and
throw you out the window!" I asked for water but they
would not give me any.

The police then tried a new tactic on the exhausted man:

They took me to my cell and told me to sit. Another
policeman came in a few minutes later and started
screaming at me that I was not allowed to sit and hit me.
Someone else came in soon after and hit me because I
was supposed to sit. This was repeated several times.

This lasted until about 9:30 P.M., when the policemen
returned with a detention warrant that I signed.

That evening, the authorities transferred Mr. Hasani to a prison
in Priština, where they left him alone until the next night. Then came
perhaps the most chilling episode in his capture:

> About 9 o'clock the next night, the prison warden had
> me handcuffed and taken to an inspector at the state
> security office. Again he told me that I should confess.
> After I refused, they took me to a room where I saw a
> man hanging from the ceiling by his feet. Two
> policemen were clubbing him and he was screaming.
> The radio was on full blast so his screams could not be
> heard. The police told me that they would beat me
> much harder than him if I did not confess.

> They took me to the fourth floor where I was beaten and
> interrogated for about two hours. They left me in a cell
> that was totally dark.

Mr. Hasani still resolved that he would rather die than confess.

> About 3:00 A.M., they came for me again. They took me
> to the state security offices where they beat me again.
> The inspector said that whoever gets into his hands has
> to confess. They took me back to my cell for a while and
> then came again for me. They beat me some more with
> clubs.

On the morning of May 24, the authorities took Mr. Hasani to
see a prison doctor. Later that day, they brought him in front of an
investigative judge, Zoran Tabaković. Mr. Hasani again stated that he
had nothing to confess.

The police left Mr. Hasani alone for about ten days, and then
brought him back to the state security offices for more beatings. At this
time, Mr. Hasani said, "One of the inspectors warned his friends not to
hit me on the face or the judge will scream." According to Mr. Hasani, he
was brought in front of the investigative judge two or three times during

his four months of detention and, after every visit to the judge, he was taken back to the police.

On July 13, 1993, Mr. Hasani was indicted for illegal possession of arms and ammunition, along with four others, Basri Islami (born in 1956), Izajedin Ajeti (born in 1965), Basri Sejdiu (born in 1963), and Bajram Rahmani (born in 1945).[39] The next day, July 14, the District Court in Priština issued an order extending the pre-trial detention of all of the men for another sixty days.[40]

While Mr. Hasani was still in prison — post-indictment and pre-trial — the police returned to search his house. His wife, Nexhmie Hasani, remembers:

> At about 2:15 in the morning on August 10, I heard someone walking around the house. I saw three uniformed policemen and one civilian. The children and I hid in the house and did not open the door when they knocked. I heard one of them say, "There is no one in the house." One of them holding a machine gun stood guard in front of the house while the others looked around for about twenty minutes.

Mrs. Hasani said that the search was very thorough:

> They even searched the trash. They took a shovel from the storage house in the yard and dug a hole in the ground. They put something in the ground that was connected to the window by a thin wire. I heard noises coming out of it. When they left, I smashed it to pieces. In another hole in the ground, they buried four small bullets. I threw them in a sewer.

On August 13, Mr. Hasani was brought to a hearing on his case in the District Court of Prizren along with other local LDK leaders who had been arrested at the same time. Mr. Hasani recalled:

---

[39] *Indictment*, dated July 13, 1993.

[40] *Extension of the Detention Document*, dated July 14, 1993, Priština.

I told the judge that I had been tortured and I wanted to take my shirt off to show the bruises. The first accused, Basri Islami, said that he had confessed under torture that he received guns from me. Mr. Islami [told the judge] that he [in fact] had only heard of me, but that he does not even know me in person.

Mr. Islami was sentenced to four years and six months in prison. Izajedin Ajeti, the second accused, was sentenced to four years. I was the third accused and I was released. ... The fourth, Bajram Rahmani, got four years.

On September 16th, 1993, Mr. Hasani was operated on for injuries sustained during his imprisonment. Since his release, he reports that he still suffers from a number of medical problems.

Police Abuse of Civilians in Response to Purported Albanian Violence

Summary of Incidents Since CSCE Withdrawal

Since the CSCE withdrawal in July 1993, Serbian police have stepped up attacks against Albanian civilians; in doing so, authorities have pointed to several recent police killings as purported justification for detaining and interrogating Albanians. One Albanian human rights worker in Uroševac voiced the sentiment of many in stating: "Police simply use any opportunity they can get to beat us. Since late July, everyone who gets interrogated at the police station is accused of having wounded a policeman."[41]

For example, on July 4, 1993, a policeman was killed at the police checkpoint entering Peć/Pejë. No one was arrested in connection with the incident. Serbian authorities claim that the death was the work of Albanian terrorists. The Chairman of the Human Rights Council of Pejë, Tahir Demaj, says "We don't know how the incident occurred, and we

---

[41] Human Rights Watch/Helsinki interview in Uroševac, October 1993. Report corroborated by numerous other interviews throughout Kosovo in September - October 1993. Name withheld to protect witness.

have no information on it."[42]   According to Mr. Demaj, police in Peć
used the incident as a pretext to raid villages surrounding Peć, beating
villagers, searching homes and detaining, interrogating and further
beating suspected village leaders.

Mr. Demaj explained what happened:

> In the morning of that day [July 4], police stopped cars
> and buses entering Pejë and people walking to work — a
> lot of people were detained and kept for several hours.
> Most were harassed in the police office, physically and
> mentally. On that day alone, police raided four villages,
> beating and threatening everyone.[43]

The Human Rights Council of Pejë estimates that police raided
approximately 300 homes on July 4, beating at least 148 people.[44]
Intensified police harassment of Albanian civilians continued on a daily
basis throughout the month, with at least a half dozen people taken into
the police station for questioning each day.[45]   This scenario was
repeated in several other villages throughout the summer and fall of
1993.

One Town Under Seige: Podujevo/Podujevë

Podujevo, a city in northern Kosovo that is ninety-nine percent
Albanian, provides an illustration of an Albanian town under seige.[46]
Long a seat of Albanian resistance, Podujevo has been the site of several

---

[42] Human Rights Watch/Helsinki interview in Peć, October 1993.

[43] Human Rights Watch/Helsinki interview in Peć, October 1993.

[44] Although Human Rights Watch/Helsinki has been unable to confirm these
figures, the incident is supported by testimony of witnesses and victims.

[45] Mr. Demaj provided numerous examples, complete with signed testimonies
and photos of people who had been beaten during the searches.

[46] Human Rights Watch/Helsinki interview with human rights activists in
Podujevo, October 1993.

demonstrations since the early 1980s. In 1993, citizens reported an increased presence of paramilitary troops and routine police harassment.[47]   One doctor interviewed in Podujevo testified, "every weekend and several days of the week, I treat people who were beaten by police."[48]   This characterization was independently confirmed by numerous victims and witnesses.

Since a police officer was shot and killed in Podujevo in July 1993, tensions have only increased. Although no one was arrested or charged in connection with the incident, the police used the killing as a pretext to step up harassment and interrogations of Albanians in and around the area.

On July 26, 1993, police raided the villages of Sekiraće/Sekiraqë and Poljonice/Polonicë, both in the vicinity of Podujevo. Purportedly the police were looking for suspects in connection with the wounding of the policeman. In both villages, large numbers of police swarmed around the villages in the early morning hours, searching houses and beating residents at random. Reportedly, police forced some of the villagers to beat each other, and commanded others to give each other piggy back rides and to engage in military exercises.[49]

An eighteen-year-old young man, Esat Ejupi, observed the raid on his village Poljonice from a safe hiding place several meters away. Mr. Ejupi explained:

> At the time the police arrived at my village, I was with my father at the mill. My father told me to stay at the mill while he went home. He started to go toward our house when a policeman saw him and shouted, "Come here." They didn't see me. When he came, one of the policemen punched him and he fell down. Then they started to beat him. There were about eight to ten of

[47] Information gathered from Human Rights Watch/Helsinki interviews with Selman Hoxha, President of the Council on Human Rights, and Bexhet Shala, member of the Presidency of the Council on Human Rights, in Podujevo, October 1993.

[48] Human Rights Watch/Helsinki interview in Podujevo, October 1993.

[49] Human Rights Watch/Helsinki interview in Podujevo, October 1993.

them. They kicked him and hit him with their fists and
with the butts of machine guns. And then they dragged
him in front of the house. After that, I couldn't see
anything anymore.[50]

While the young man hid at the mill, the police raided his house
and other homes in the village. The villagers estimate that about 300
policemen took part in the raid, beating over 100 people, arresting about
thirty men, and searching a total of forty-eight (out of ninety) houses.

Esad's seventy-three-year-old grandfather, Maliq Ejupi, was in the
first house raided by the police:

On July 26 at 7:00 A.M., I was lying in this bed here.
The police came in my house. They entered my room.
In my room there were plenty of them and in the yard
in front of the house, there were about seventy
policemen. They had police uniforms and machine guns.
When they entered, they said "Are you sleeping?" I said,
"I am old, tired and sick and I cannot get up early in the
morning." One of them said, "I will make you get up
early now!"

This policeman saw that I had on my wall a picture of
Rugova [the Albanian leader], my son who had been
killed in the demonstration and an Albanian symbol. He
pointed to my son and demanded to know who he was.
I said, "That's my son." He asked me where he is, and I
said that he had been killed. ... And then he asked me,
"Who killed him?" I said, "The police did." And he asked
again, "Why?" And I answered that he was killed during
the demonstrations in Podujevo [in 1989]. After that,
another policeman said to this first one, "This is the
man." Then the first policeman hit the picture of
Rugova with his rifle butt and broke it. The same
policeman came here and hit me with a stick on the
head. I fell down and lost consciousness. What

---

[50] Human Rights Watch/Helsinki interview in Poljonice, October 1993.

happened next, I don't know, but I know from my
injuries that they beat me hard on my back.[51]

While Mr. Ejupi remained unconscious, police tore his house
apart, shattering the photo of his dead son, breaking furniture, and
scattering belongings across the floor. The police took two of Mr. Ejupi's
sons, Isa, a thirty-four-year-old former policeman, and Idriz, thirty-one
years old, into the station for questioning. Mr. Ejupi remembered:

After I was beaten, I couldn't walk. I could take just two
or three steps. I was dizzy. I'm still a little dizzy now
[one and a half months after the incident].

Mr. Ejupi added that the police stole a very expensive typewriter from his
house.
M.K., a doctor who treated several of the villagers after the
incident testified that one man had broken ribs, another a broken hand,
and several had severe bruises. According to this doctor, "No one had
open wounds. It seems that the police make sure that people don't
bleed."[52]
Some of the villagers stated that after the raid they found a
"Četnik"[53] symbol in a house that had apparently fallen off one of the

---

[51] Human Rights Watch/Helsinki interview in Poljonice, October 1993.

[52] Human Rights Watch/Helsinki interview in Poljonice, October 1993. Name
withheld to protect witness.

[53] During the Second World War, the Četniks fought against the occupying
Axis powers and called for the restoration of the Serbian monarchy and the
creation of a Greater Serbia. The Četniks also fought against the pro-Nazi Ustaša
forces of Croatia and Tito's communist Partisans and committed atrocities against
Muslims and Croats, primarily in Bosnia-Hercegovina. Croats and Muslims both
in Croatia and Bosnia-Hercegovina commonly refer to Serbian military and
paramilitary forces engaged in the current wars in Croatia and Bosnia-
Hercegovina as "Četniks." The Yugoslav army and some Serbian paramilitary
groups vehemently reject the label "Četnik," claiming that they are merely
defenders of their people and their land and that they are not extremists.
Others, such as paramilitary units loyal to the ultra-right wing leader of the
Serbian Radical Party, Vojislav Šešelj, commonly refer to themselves as Četniks.

policemen's uniforms, thus indicating possible paramilitary involvement
in the raid.[54]

Another incident that could be attributed to the heightened
tensions in Podujevo was the police killing of a twenty-two-year-old
Albanian, Mehdi Maksuti. Mehdi, his brother Ahmet (twenty-eight years
old), and another friend, Shaban, had been driving in the early morning
hours through Podujevo when the tragic incident occurred. Police shot
at their car, allegedly because they had run a stop sign. But, according
to Mehdi's other brother, Afrim, there was no stop sign.

After Mehdi had been hit, Shaban drove to the brother's house,
in the village of Shtedim, near Podujevo, to get help. Afrim testified:

> They came to the house and got me, and we carried
> Mehdi out of the car. We put him in another car and
> drove to the hospital in Priština. My older brother,
> Ahmet, stayed in the hospital with him and I returned
> home. At 11:00 A.M., the police came to search our
> house. There were about twenty of them, dressed in full
> gear — wearing flak jackets, helmets and armed with
> machine guns. They arrived in an armored personnel
> carrier and three or four cars.[55]

Afrim said that the police did not mistreat his mother and sister,
but during the search,

> The police planted a gun in the house and "found it."
> They then said, "Why don't you admit that this is your
> revolver?" We said, "Because it is not ours!" They
> answered, "How dare you say something like that?!"
> They then beat me a little. Two of them hit me with
> fists and one of them kicked me.

---

[54] The villagers also testified that policemen later told them that the men who
had raided their homes were not, for the most part, local police, but some local
police joined in.

[55] Human Rights Watch/Helsinki interview in Podujevo, October 1993.

The police took Afrim to the police station in Podujevo, where he was joined by his brother Ahmet. It was at this point that Afrim learned that Mehdi had died. Police interrogated Afrim and Ahmet together. Afrim remembered:

> They asked us about the revolver and where we got it. They threatened that they would not let us go to our brother's funeral unless we told them where we got the gun. They eventually released us about 1:00 A.M..

Although the police promised Afrim that they would be back at his house again soon, as of this writing they have not yet returned for him.

Evictions of Albanians From Their Homes

In at least three reported cases,[56] police officers in the area of Mitrovica have harassed families into leaving their homes so that Serbs could inhabit them. One woman, E.F., told her story:

> On the 25th of July at about 6 A.M., I suddenly heard a knock on my door. My husband wasn't home. He was visiting a sick relative from his village. At that moment, I thought maybe the relative had died and that my husband had come home. When I opened the door, the first thing I saw was a machine gun in front of my face. There were three uniformed policemen standing there with their guns.
>
> One of the policemen asked, "Where is your husband?" And I said, "He is not home." He asked me, "Who is the owner of this apartment?" I told him that I was, and he said, "Look woman, I give you twenty-four hours to get out of this apartment." He told me that he was a Serbian refugee from Bosnia and that he needed my apartment. I asked him why I must leave — it was my place. He said, "I don't care where you go. Just leave and I will come

---

[56] Information gathered from Human Rights Watch/Helsinki interviews in Kosovo, September-October, 1993.

here to live, otherwise you will regret it if I find you here
after twenty-four hours." All the time he was speaking,
he was pointing his gun at me and during that time, they
insulted me as a woman and as an Albanian.[57]

After waiting for her husband for two hours, the police officers
left E.F.'s home, only to return again and again:

From that day, for the next twenty days or so, they
would come every day. Each time they were wearing
different uniforms — sometimes police uniforms,
sometimes some other uniforms, sometimes civilian
clothes. Just the person who was interested in the
apartment was the same. Every time he brought one or
two others.

E.F. had worked before in the civilian branch of the local police station,
so she usually knew the local police officers by name. Still, she did not
recognize any of the men who came to her door.
　　One day, E.F. tried to report the incident to the chief inspector
of the local police. According to E.F., the officer "said that he didn't
know anything about the case and he told me to go home." When E.F.
returned home, she learned from her daughters that the policeman had
been in her home in her absence. They returned later, the same day:

At about 12:15 P.M., the same policeman came back with
two other policemen in regular police uniforms. ... They
pushed me aside and came into my house by force. They
said, "Why don't you start packing?" I said, "I will not
pack, because I was at the police station and the chief
inspector said that I must stay in my apartment." He
accused me of lying. I told him, "You should be
ashamed. I am maybe two times your age and you tell
me that I'm lying."

---

[57] Human Rights Watch/Helsinki interview in Mitrovica, September 1993.
Name withheld to protect witness.

> I grabbed the phone and called the chief inspector. He
> told me to put one of the men on the phone. The man
> that was interested in my flat took the phone and started
> to threaten the chief inspector. He yelled into the
> receiver, "I will go to Belgrade and tell them that you are
> supporting Albanians here."

The men eventually left E.F.'s home. At 4:00 P.M. that afternoon,
the man who was interested in the apartment returned again, this time
alone and in civilian clothes. According to E.F., this time his threats
intensified:

> He told me that he had to talk to me privately, so he had
> my children get out. When we were alone, he
> threatened to rape and kill me. ... He said, "I can rape
> and I can kill you and you can't complain to anyone. I
> can do it because I am Serbian. The only thing they can
> do to me is to change my job, to give me a promotion."
> ... He also said, "You know, I can do something else. I
> can go into a restaurant in a place where everyone will
> see me and have a drink while I send someone else to
> rape and kill you and your girls. I would have a perfect
> alibi."

Too afraid to stay any longer, E.F. vacated the apartment.
Reportedly another policeman (not the man claiming to be from Bosnia),
now lives in E.F.'s apartment. E.F. and her family are living doubled up
with relatives.

Raids on Albanian Shops and Market Places

Numerous Albanians throughout Kosovo reported police
interference with their commercial establishments.[58]   In a typical
scenario, police raid an Albanian store and demand all of the cash on
hand. As Ismajl Kelmendi, an Albanian clerk in Peć explained:

---

[58] Information gathered from Human Rights Watch/Helsinki interviews in
Kosovo, September-October 1993.

On September 6th at 1:55 in the afternoon, two
members of the state security in plain clothes came to the
shop where I work and asked for hard currency. I had
about 800 [German] marks, but they were hidden. They
had no warrant. I looked to my uncle for some kind of
signal telling me what I should do. The cop saw my look
and he hit me across my face. He tried to hit me again,
but I grabbed his arm and stopped him. He shouted, "I'll
kill you! I'll kill you!" and he went for his gun, but again
I stopped him. The other policeman came over, and my
uncle yelled, "Kill, kill, so we see you can kill!" ... They
searched around and found our money. They took me to
the police station, but they wouldn't talk to me ... After
they kept me there for about one and a half hours, they
gave me a slip of paper saying they had taken my
money, but they warned me, "Don't ask for this, or you'll
get in trouble."[59]

The President of the LDK in Gnjilane, Basri Musmurati, similarly
stated:

If you compare the situation here to when the CSCE was
here, it is worse than it was then. From the day [the
CSCE] left, the oppression has become more prevalent
and brutal. ... The most typical case is that people are
robbed by the Serbian police, especially the so-called
fiscal police. Private companies owned by Albanians are
the biggest targets. In September, for example, the
police stole 150,000 [German] marks from one
company.[60]

In addition to raids for hard currency, several Albanians,
particularly jewelry store clerks and owners, reported incidents in which
police simply took whatever precious goods they wanted. No one
reported any success at retrieving their goods and, in fact, most

---

[59] Human Rights Watch/Helsinki interview in Peć, October 1993.

[60] Human Rights Watch/Helsinki interview in Gnjilane, October 1993.

shopkeepers reported that they were too afraid to even try to get them back.

The LDK President in Peć, Ymer Muhaxheri, said that this reluctance was natural:

> The pressure is continuous. Police expeditions, raids on villages, armed civilians parading around. They always use weapon searches as excuses. They harass families and beat parents in front of their children. Very rarely are there no incidents. Here, in town, the repression takes an uglier form. They use fiscal controls, tax controls to break the Albanian shop owners. They surround one part of the town and search everyone to collect hard currency. No one dares react. There is no contact between the citizens and the government.[61]

Police harassment of Albanian civilians appears to be particularly brutal in Peć, where many citizens testified as to nearly daily raids on marketplaces. One man spoke for many:

> The police charge into the marketplace whenever they want and search everyone. Last Saturday, they blocked seven streets and searched everyone who was there. They took everything that people were selling. I was in a little bar near the market at the time. Policemen entered the place and said, "Put everything you have on the table!" They were wearing police uniforms and they had machine guns. I had twenty [German] marks on me, and they took it. Because I'm a little older, they didn't bother much with me. But I saw them hitting and harassing some of the other guys.[62]

Not all elderly people are so lucky: on November 13, 1993, in Priština, Human Rights Watch/Helsinki representatives interviewed a

---

[61] Human Rights Watch/Helsinki interview in Peć, October 1993.

[62] Human Rights Watch/Helsinki interview in Peć, October 1993. Name withheld to protect witness.

feeble old man, Rashit Murati, seventy-seven years old, an illiterate
farmer from a village near Podujevo. Mr. Murati needed help walking
and his face was covered with dried blood. He recounted what had
happened to him:

> I left the mosque (in Podujevo) at about 1:00 P.M. today
> and started towards the car where my family was waiting
> for me. At this moment, the police were raiding the
> market and were chasing the children who were selling
> cigarettes. I turned into a narrow street and found
> myself surrounded by four or five policemen. They
> started hitting me — I do not know with what. I fainted
> and woke up in the police station.[63]

When Mr. Murati came to at the police station, the officers
accused him of having started a fight with them.

> One of the policemen spoke some Albanian and he
> insisted that I tell them why I had attacked the officers.
> The commander of the [police] station asked me the
> same thing. I said that I didn't say anything or hit
> anyone, that I only tried to hide.

> About an hour later, Miloš Nikolić, a policeman from the
> village of Surkišc/Surkish (near Podujevo), took my
> statement. He did not read it to me, and I had to
> imprint it with my thumb. Eventually, he told me that I
> could leave. I said that I could not walk and that I
> needed a doctor. At that, Nikolić tore up my statement
> and some policemen carried me to the entrance of the
> police station. Some people then took me to my son's
> house. By this time, it was about 3:30 P.M..

Mr. Murati's son inquired at the police station several times
during those two and a half hours about his father's whereabouts. They
told him that they were not holding him. The doctor who examined Mr.

---

[63] Human Rights Watch/Helsinki interview in Priština, November 13, 1993.

Murati immediately upon his release found an open wound on his forehead as a result of a blow with a blunt object. Similar reports from throughout Kosovo paint a picture of continual tension and turmoil, communities under seige.

RESTRICTIONS ON FREEDOM OF ASSOCIATION

Although the Constitution of the Federal Republic of Yugoslavia (Articles 40 and 41)[1] guarantee "the freedom of assembly and other peaceful gathering" as well as "the freedom of political, trade union and other association," the police frequently harass members of Albanian organizations and raid meetings of Albanians in Kosovo. The following section highlights the nature and scope of the harassment.

HARASSMENT OF HUMAN RIGHTS GROUPS

In addition to human rights observers working under the auspices of the political parties — particularly those associated with the Democratic League of Kosovo (LDK) — there are two local human rights organizations in Kosovo: The Council for the Defense of Human Rights and Freedoms ("the Council"), formed in 1989[2], and the Kosova Helsinki Committee, formed in 1990 and accepted as an affiliated member of the International Helsinki Federation (IHF) in 1993. The Council, the more active of the two groups, has a base office in Priština, which publishes detailed and, to Human Rights Watch/Helsinki's knowledge, accurate bulletins, and coordinates the work of Albanians in smaller towns and villages.

The authorities have tolerated the existence of these organizations, even allowing the Council to register officially. Nonetheless, police continually harass members, pulling them in for frequent "informative talks," arrests and beatings. The Council reports that the harassment has not abated over time but, if anything, has grown more random and severe.

On July 7, 1993, police raided the headquarters of the Council, taking with them, among other materials, eighteen videotapes and all of

---

[1] *Constitution of the Federal Republic of Yugoslavia*, Belgrade, 1992.

[2] The Council is also known as the "Office for the Protection and Defense of Human Rights."

the court documents on the premises.[3] Adem Demaqi, the leader of the Council was present:

> I heard that something was happening, so I went to the Council. As I was going into the courtyard, I saw police. They said, "Where are you going?" I said, "I work here." I walked past them and into the office. I saw about four or five Council members and about the same number of police. I asked, "Where is your warrant?" One of the police pointed to his uniform and said "This is my warrant." I could see that the police had one of the Council member's hands tied. One of the police pointed to me and said, "You're enemy number one!"[4]

Demaqi stated that he tried to have the police arrest him as the leader of the Council. However, the police pushed him away, saying "You're an old man!" Instead of Demaqi, police took another member of the Council, Sami Kurteshi, to the police station in Priština. Because Mr. Kurteshi has since fled from Kosovo, Demaqi testified as to his treatment:

> I saw him the day after they took him in. They had beaten him so badly that he couldn't walk. They beat him particularly bad on the soles of his feet. After they were through with him, they literally dumped him in front of the police station door. Someone passing by found him there and took him to the hospital. His bones were not broken because he was beaten professionally. Still, he was so badly bruised that he had difficulty walking. He later fled to Switzerland.

The police left official receipts for the video tapes and other material that they took from the Council headquarters. However, despite

---

[3] See *Charges Against the Illegal Search of the Office for the Protection and Defense of Human Rights in Priština by Police*, July 20, 1993, Priština.

[4] Human Rights Watch/Helsinki interview in Priština, September 1993.

Demaqi's repeated visits to the police station to demand the goods,[5] the police have never returned any of their belongings.

Demaqi and other Council members describe the current situation as one of tenuous state toleration. "The police have never come here to close us down for good. They could do it, but they don't," Demaqi said. "Instead, they leave us here to show to foreign delegations." However, Demaqi emphasized, the police keep harassing them on a regular basis "to let us know what they could do to us whenever they want."[6]

Human rights activists in other parts of Kosovo have reported similar raids and arrests. Adem Salihaj — the president of the Human Rights Council for Ferizaj and a deputy in the Kosova Assembly[7] — was arrested after a house search on September 16, 1993 at 5:30 A.M.. Sanije Aliu, a member of the presidency of the LDK in Uroševac explained:

> They took him to a police station in Uroševac. They kept him there for three days before they told the family where he was. On September 18, they transferred him to the Priština District Prison. The lawyers saw him for the first time there on September 22 and they saw that he had been brutally beaten. Adem asked his lawyers to alert the public that he had been tortured both in Ferizaj and in Priština. He also told them that he was interrogated by the police for 10 days before they took him to an investigative judge.[8]

---

[5] See *The Request for the Documentation to be Submitted*, August 2, 1993, Priština (request by Demaqi for goods to be returned).

[6] Human Rights Watch/Helsinki interview in Priština, September 1993.

[7] On May 24, 1992, ethnic Albanians in Kosovo held elections in which they voted for representatives to a clandestine Albanian parliament and government. Serbian authorities declared the voting to be illegal. Most Albanians abide by the decisions of this shadow government and refuse to accept Belgrade's direct rule over Kosovo, in which they claim not to be represented.

[8] Human Rights Watch/Helsinki interview in Uroševac, October 1993.

When Ms. Aliu saw Mr. Salihaj for the first time on September 28, she was shocked at his condition:

> Adem was crossing from the car into the court building [when I saw him]. I barely recognized him although we had worked together for a long time. He was walking with difficulty and he appeared very weary. Two policemen supported him when he walked.

Mr. Salihaj, like most human rights activists arrested in Kosovo, was charged with violating the territorial integrity of Yugoslavia. On its face, his case appears unrelated to his activities at the Human Rights Council, as the charges do not mention the Council. Instead, Mr. Salihaj was accused of being a commander of the local military headquarters and plotting a rebellion.

Foreign humanitarian and human rights workers have also faced attempts to block and/or disrupt their work. In the fall of 1993, for example, the Serbian government refused to issue a visa to Amnesty International after it learned of the group's plans to travel to Kosovo.

In addition, police detained and interrogated a Human Rights Watch/Helsinki representative attending a trial in Prizren with permission of the court (for the details of the trial, see below). The Human Rights Watch/Helsinki representative was waiting in front of the court house after the trial for a British television journalist who could give her a ride back to Priština. She remembered:

> We were approached by four or five uniformed men with machine guns. They told us to get into a police car. I argued that I would not do so without a warrant or at least an explanation as to why we were being summoned. After one of them grumbled that the police commander wanted to see us, we agreed to go with them.[9]

The armed police drove them to the main police station in Prizren. There, the Human Rights Watch/Helsinki representative recalled:

---

[9] Statement by Human Rights Watch/Helsinki representative, November 1993.

Three plain-clothes policemen interrogated us together
for about ten minutes before they told [the British
journalist] that she was free to go. Concerned for me,
she insisted on staying. I learned later that after she had
insisted on staying, they kept her for almost three hours
and confiscated her tapes. ...

I was ordered to go to another room, where I spent the
next four hours with a man who refused to identify
himself. ... The man who conducted most of the
interrogation played the "good cop," trying to chat
casually when the others were not around. They accused
me of working for an anti-Serb organization. ... They
also insisted on my disclosing the identities of my
contacts in Kosovo and how much I get paid. ... The
police station commander stormed in repeatedly and
screamed threats at me.

After four hours had passed, under pressure from foreign journalists and
the U.S. Embassy, who had been notified by the lawyers of those on trial,
the police let the Human Rights Watch/Helsinki representative go.

HARASSMENT OF INDIVIDUALS WHO MEET WITH
OR AID FOREIGN DELEGATIONS

The CSCE (Conference on Security and Cooperation in Europe)
set up a long-term human rights mission in Kosovo in September 1992
with the acquiescence of the federal government. Serbian authorities
despite Montenegrin objections and the U.N. Security Council's
resolution calling for the mission's continuation, expelled the CSCE
monitors in July 1993. Immediately thereafter, police began
interrogating and harassing Albanians who had acted as guides,
interpreters and/or hosts for the CSCE. Though the treatment of those
brought in for questioning varied, some of the former aides to the CSCE
reported that they were held for prolonged periods and/or beaten.

One such case involved Masar Shporta a professor in Prizren who
had rented part of his home to two CSCE monitors. On August 7, 1993,
at 8:00 A.M., Mr. Shporta was riding his bicycle near his home when he

was stopped by police. Without offering a reason, the police officers directed him to go to the police station. Mr. Shporta recounted:

> They took me to the office of the state security and put me in a small room where they interrogated me. ... They accused me of terrorism. ... I'm a member of the LDK of this municipal district. They also wanted to talk about that. They wanted all the details on the meetings — who's present, what they say, etc. After this, they showed me some party program of a party that I had never heard of, some party "for the Republic of Kosovo." I told them, "I didn't read this outside your office, I'm not reading it here."

> One young man was quite decent — he played the good cop — but his boss would come in and out and threaten to beat me, but they never did, maybe because I'm an old man. But they tried to force me to sign that I was a member of this party. ... This lasted until about 10:00 P.M.. Then they put me in a small room that wasn't like a place any human being should be in. The air was very bad and I could hardly breathe.[10]

The police didn't allow the professor to call his family, nor could he phone a lawyer.

Worried about their father's disappearance, Mr. Shporta's family checked local hospitals and police stations for him. His daughter said that at the police station, the officers simply said, "We don't hold old people here. This isn't an old folks home." She said that she finally learned of his whereabouts through unofficial channels at about 9:00 P.M. on the day he disappeared.

The next day, the interrogation continued:

> All day, they wanted to know about the same organization for the Republic of Kosovo. They claimed that this organization was a section of the LDK. Also,

---

[10] Human Rights Watch/Helsinki interviews in Prizren, September 1993 and January 1994.

they wanted to know about the [Albanian] university and they insulted the university, saying nothing good could be in Albanian. The guy playing the good cop was doing the interrogation while another cop would keep coming in and out. They didn't beat me. But they would do things like take my glasses off so I couldn't see, and hold my neck with their hands like they would strangle me. But they didn't do it. ... They also threatened to set me up for killing two police officers.

According to Mr. Shporta, one line of questioning involved the CSCE monitors:

They asked me about the CSCE people who had stayed at my house. They wanted to know if they write to me, if I spent a lot of time with them when they were here. They wanted to know what they were looking for when they were here. I told them that I don't speak English, that the most communicating we did was in sign language.

That night, the police brought the professor to the regular police station. The next day, a Monday, the interrogation continued along the same line as the day before. This time, however, the policemen took down his statement and forced him to rewrite everything that they had said he said. Monday night they put him in a cell at the regular police station.

On Tuesday morning, the police left the professor alone in his cell. Instead, they turned their attention to his home. According to the professor's son, about twenty police officers arrived at his house that day in full riot gear:

You should have seen them. They surrounded the house like they were apprehending someone very dangerous, just like a movie. They searched everything from about 10:00 A.M. until 1:00 P.M.. They took some things — my father's and mother's passports.[11] They took an auto map of Europe and Turkey. ... We asked them for a search warrant, and they wrote one down for us.[12]

That afternoon, the interrogation of the professor continued, but this time they questioned him about a new subject. Apparently, a young doctor who had been arrested earlier in the day had told the police that a group of Albanians was storing medicine in the professor's house. According to the professor, some people had collected money for medicines for the poor, but the medicines were not being stored at his house. Indeed, the police search of his house failed to uncover any medicines. The professor tried to explain the situation to the police for about five hours before he was taken back to his prison cell.

The next day, the police took the professor before an investigative judge to secure permission to detain him longer. According to the professor:

> The whole procedure lasted five or ten minutes. There was a lawyer there who had been retained by my family. That was the first time I had a chance to speak with him. It was very quick and that was that. I was back in my cell.
>
> The next day, my lawyer came to the prison for the first time to ask if I needed anything. He had a paper with him that said I could be kept for thirty more days.

On the 15th of August, over a week after the arrest, the professor's family was allowed to visit with him briefly. On August 18, the professor's lawyer appealed the order granting the police permission to hold him for an additional thirty days. He was released on the same day, but the charges were not dropped for another month. However, in November the authorities re-opened Mr. Shporta's case. With no apparent new evidence, he was again accused of jeopardizing the

---

[11] At the date of the interview, the couple had still not received their passports back, despite repeated trips to the police station.

[12] Human Rights Watch/Helsinki interview in Prizren, September 1993.

territorial integrity of Yugoslavia, a violation of Article 116, paragraph
1 of the Yugoslav Criminal Code.

Another Albanian recently arrested after meeting with foreign
delegations is Muhamet Shukriu, a sixty-seven-year-old professor and
activist for Albanian culture and for the repatriation of Albanians who
have emigrated from Kosovo. Mr. Shukriu was arrested on September
29, 1993, one day after he met with representatives from the British
Embassy. His wife, Margarita Shukriu, explained what happened:

> One uniformed and one plainclothes police officer came
> to our door at about 7:45 in the morning. I was asleep
> and my husband came to wake me up. He said only,
> "They came to get me." ... He said goodbye to me. I
> gave him a jacket to bring with him. I held the jacket
> for him as he put it on. ... The uniformed police officer
> held a machine gun in his hand, pointing it to the floor.
> I thought there was nothing to discuss because I didn't
> want to get them nervous.[13]

Less than an hour after the police had taken her husband away,
a group of nine policemen — six in uniform and three in civilian clothing
— returned to Mrs. Shukriu's home. Starting with the basement and the
garage, the policemen searched the Shukriu home thoroughly. A couple
of hours later, after they finished rummaging through Mr. Shukriu's
home office, an officer filled out two documents: first, a search warrant
granting them permission to "look through the premises" with the stated
purpose that "objects and propaganda material of the [unspecified]
offense will be found," and, second, a receipt for confiscated property.
Although he filled the documents out at the same time, the officer dated
the first document for "September 29, 11:00 A.M.," and the second
document for "September 29, 9:00 A.M.." Mrs. Shukriu noted this
incongruity:

> I told them I thought that according to law they should
> have given me a warrant at the door, not after they were
> done searching. They said, "This is the way we do it." ...

---

[13] Human Rights Watch/Helsinki interview in Prizren, September 1993.

> I told them that I wouldn't let them take a big pile of
> papers and books without listing everything separately.
> They said, "That's not our custom. We're taking all of
> this to your husband and he'll explain what is what."

After the police left, Mr. Shukriu's family tried to find out what
had happened to him. For four days, the police didn't allow Mr. Shukriu
to call either his family or a lawyer. According to Mr. Shukriu's son, who
was interviewed while his father was still being held:

> I went back and forth to the police station nonstop for
> four days and I couldn't get anything. Officially, they
> didn't want to tell me anything. They didn't even want
> to talk to me. I finally got a cop that I know to give me
> some information. He told me that my father is in
> prison. I went to look for him in the prison and again
> they wouldn't give me any information. An Albanian
> prison guard whom I know confirmed that they had
> brought him there. The guard said that my father wasn't
> listed as if he was ever brought into the police station,
> because the secret police are in charge of the case. ...
> The regular police don't know anything. They let me
> look in their books to show that he's not listed there.[14]

Mr. Shukriu's daughter, also interviewed while her father was
being held, added:

> We've consulted a lawyer, and he hasn't been able to get
> in touch with my father. He's gone each day to the
> police, but there is a total blockage of information. ...
> We're especially worried because his health isn't good
> and he's always said that he would start a hunger strike
> if the police ever kept him for more than a day.[15]

---

[14] Human Rights Watch/Helsinki interview in Prizren, September 1993.

[15] Human Rights Watch/Helsinki interview in Prizren, September 1993.

After holding Mr. Shukriu for four days at the police station, authorities transferred him to prison on October 2. He was released the following day. He later told Human Rights Watch/Helsinki that at the police station he had been "held in a chair cuffed to a radiator. Different inspectors interrogated and threatened me."[16] According to Mr. Shukriu, he had been interrogated from 7:30 A.M. until 11:00 P.M. for three days straight.

> They wanted to know what I had told the British Embassy delegation. I said that I had told them that the only solution for the Kosovo problem is negotiations between the Serbs and the Albanians, under international mediation. The police said that I would never leave the station.
>
> All of a sudden, they wanted me to "confess" that I was the chief commander of the paramilitary formations that are trained in Albania. They claimed that they had five people who had testified against me.[17]

Mr. Shukriu identified some of the inspectors who had interrogated him as Mika Jovanović, Vjekoslav Jović, Lulzim Neziri and Latif Duha. Station commander Milivoje Savić also frequently entered the office and asked questions.

HARASSMENT OF POLITICAL ORGANIZATIONS

Albanian Organizations

Claiming more than 600,000 "members and sympathizers" out of population of 1.2 million adults, the Democratic Alliance of Kosova (LDK) is the largest Albanian party in Kosovo. LDK leader Ibrahim Rugova is also the elected president of the "illegal" Albanian government

---

[16] Human Rights Watch/Helsinki interview in Prizren, December 1993.

[17] *Id.*

of Kosova.[18] Due to its dominant position in Albanian politics, the LDK has become so closely identified with the Albanian government that, Rugova himself notes, "it's more of a movement" than a party.

Rugova reports that while police have kept him under constant surveillance and, over the years, continually harassed and detained him for "informative talks," they save the worst abuse for his deputies and other lower level political leaders. "They're just waiting for me to explode," he explained.[19]

Several members of LDK chapters reported that police had taken them in to the station for "informative talks," at times beating them and holding them for prolonged periods without counsel and without being able to notify their families as to their whereabouts.[20] Other parties[21] have reported similar incidents of harassment. Indeed, much of the testimony throughout each section of this report is from political activists.

An LDK officer in Prizren, fifty-five-year-old Salajdin Braha, testified as to a typical scenario:

> On the 7th of August, at 9:45 in the morning, I was going to the LDK officers and two people in civilian clothing were there waiting for me. When they saw me, they called me by name. They brought their car and

---

[18] As noted previously, "Kosova" is the Albanian term for Kosovo.

[19] Human Rights Watch/Helsinki interview in Priština, October 1993.

[20] For example, Ymer Muhaxheri, president of the LDK branch in Peć, was arrested on September 29, 1993 and held for several hours.

[21] There are approximately twenty non-Serbian political parties in Kosovo. Other political parties include, but are not limited to, the following: The Parliamentary Party of Kosova (PPK); The Social Democratic Party of Kosova (PSDK); The Farmers' Party of Kosova (PFK); The Albanian Christian Democratic Party of Kosova (PSHDK); The Republican Party of Kosova (PRK); The Albanian Republican Party (PRSH); The Liberal Party of Kosova (PLK); The Albanian People's Party (PPSH); The Albanian National Democratic Party (PNDSH); The Green Party of Kosova (PGJK) and The Party of Democratic Action (PAD, or SDA — Stranka Demokratske Akcije, the main political party representing Muslims in the former Yugoslavia, particularly in Bosnia-Hercegovina). Only the LDK and the Farmers' Party have been able to register officially with the authorities.

they told me to go inside. I asked them why. They said,
"Just go inside and don't anything. From that place, they
brought me into the state security offices. ... When I went
inside, their first question was, "Where is your machine
gun and your pistol?" I answered that I don't have a
machine gun and a pistol, and they said that I had been
born with them. I answered that I can't bear a gun.[22]

Mr. Braha had weekly contact with the CSCE human rights
monitors when they were in the country. The police officers questioned
him about those meetings:

They asked me whether I had contacted anyone from the
CSCE since they had left. ... They said, "Is it true that the
LDK has been contacting them regularly?" ... They were
interested in what kind of information the LDK gave the
CSCE while they were here and since they've left. I
explained to them our procedure. ... Another question
was, "Why do you check the movements of our police and
army?" I answered, "We do that because we are afraid
and we are unarmed." The policeman asked why we
were afraid that they would do something to us. I said
that we were afraid of a massacre. I explained that we're
not just afraid of the police, we're also afraid of
paramilitary forces because we had seen them.

The police were proud that they had kicked the CSCE
out of Kosovo. They bragged about it and said, "Now
you don't have the CSCE here and there is no one to
defend you."

Police kept Mr. Braha in the state security offices for three days
without anything to eat. Throughout the entire time, he was
interrogated, beaten, and forced to either sit or stand:

---

[22] Human Rights Watch/Helsinki interview in Prizren, September 1993.

The second phase of this interrogation was an attempt to force me to declare that I was a member of the Movement for the Liberation of Kosovo [a radical movement not connected with the LDK]. "With force or without force, you're going to confess this," they said. The party does not legally exist. ... They wanted me to confess to illegal activity. They told me that I was engaged in illegal activity and that I know where Albanians are training to become terrorists, and that I know where illegal weapons are stored. They said that if there was a war, I would be in charge of it. None of these things are true, so I didn't accept any of their allegations.

According to Mr. Braha, after every series of questions, the police officers used force:

When they wanted me to confess, they beat me. They hit me with police clubs, on the hand, arms and legs. On the first day, I fell from the blows and fainted. I think they called a doctor because I woke up in the next room in a bed. They took my blood pressure and gave me shots. I don't know how long this all lasted, probably a couple of hours and then the doctor said that they should take me to the hospital. I spent the first night in a civilian hospital guarded by police. They poured water on me to keep me from passing out, but I did anyway. I don't know what they did to me at the hospital.

The police did not inform Mr. Braha's family that they had him in custody. However, a friend of the family saw him at the hospital and informed his wife. Even though she went to the hospital to see him, they didn't let her in the room.

The next morning, the police took Mr. Braha back to the offices of the state security. At this point, Mr. Braha was so weak from his beating, which had apparently aggravated a previously existing high blood pressure condition, that he could hardly function.

> I told them that I didn't feel good and that I have high
> blood pressure. The police told me that I was faking it.
> They said, "You Albanians are actors and criminals."
> They interrogated me for about five hours, but I couldn't
> communicate anymore. They let me sit down. I felt
> faint and I was not able to think, to speak, to do
> anything. I had vertigo, I was dizzy and my vision was
> blurry.

In the afternoon, a couple of police officers helped Mr. Braha
walk to a cell. They kept him in the state security offices for three days
before transferring him to the regular prison. Only then, after three days
in prison, did they allow him to see a doctor and to phone his family. On
the first day in the regular prison — four days after his arrest — his family
was allowed to bring him medicine.

Mr. Braha's health improved after he took his medication, but he
was in great pain from the beatings:

> While I was in prison, my hands were swollen and dark
> black from all of the beatings. It took twelve days for my
> hands to heal. I kept them in cold water as much as I
> could.

Mr. Braha said that on the day he arrived in the regular prison,
an officer handed him a document that purported to give the authorities
permission to hold him for thirty days in prison. Mr. Braha said that he
had not seen either a judge or a lawyer before he was given this
document.

On the 12th of August, five days after his arrest, police brought
Mr. Braha before an investigative judge. The accusation claimed that Mr.
Braha was a terrorist. Mr. Braha denied the charges. According to Mr.
Braha, "We were there for a total of ten minutes and then they ordered
that I be tied up and brought back to prison."

After his appearance before the judge, Mr. Braha spent a total of
seventeen days in solitary confinement in conditions that he described as
inhumane:

> I was in a little, dark room that had only a tiny, high
> window. No one talked to me for seventeen days and I

was all alone. Then, they put me in another room with three others. If you had to go to the bathroom, you had to call a guard and he would bring you a bucket for a toilet, or you could wait until the one or two times a day when they let you go to a real toilet. Once every two weeks they let you have a shower. The food was barely edible — beans, rice and peas, no meat. And, as long as you weren't in solitary confinement, you could walk in the prison yard twice a day for 15 minutes.

On September 13, 1993, Mr. Braha was released from prison. According to Mr. Braha, "they simply gave me a document that said my case no longer exists."

Shaban Manaj, a lawyer and president of the Istok/Istog chapter of the LDK recounted another experience typical of Albanian political activists — being hauled into the police station for "informative talks."

At 8:30 A.M. on November 11 [1993], I got a phone call telling me to report to the police station in ten minutes for an "informative talk." As soon as I entered the police station [in Istok], two state security inspectors pushed me in the car and drove me to the police station in Peć.[23]

Mr. Manaj was interrogated between 9:00 A.M. and 5:45 P.M. by five inspectors who rotated every hour.

They said that the LDK had formed a National Defense Ministry of the Republic of Kosovo, which was preparing for war and had formed military units. They wanted me to "confess" to being a member of the defense ministry as well as the Territorial Defense Headquarters. They claimed that they had evidence and witnesses who testified against me. I didn't sign anything because none of this is true.

---

[23] Human Rights Watch/Helsinki interview in Priština, November 1993. At the time of this interview, Mr. Manaj still had bruises on his hands, shoulders and head.

After a while, Mr. Manaj testified, the "talks" grew violent.

> At 4:00 P.M. they started to use force, hitting me for the
> first time: one plainclothes inspector started clubbing
> and hitting me with his fists over my head, shoulders and
> hands. I received about fifteen strong blows with a
> truncheon over the palms of my hands. Meanwhile, the
> other inspector was shouting at me: "Confess, or you'll be
> arrested and charged with a serious offense!" Still, I
> would not confess. ... At about 5:15, they gave up.

Numerous additional Albanian political activists throughout
Kosovo have reported similar incidents of "informative talks" and
detention.

Turkish Organizations

Leaders of Turkish organizations in Kosovo report similar
difficulties as those encountered by their Albanian counterparts.
Approximately 20,000 Turks live in Kosovo today, approximately one
percent of the population.[24]
According to Sezair Shaipi, the head of the Turkish Peoples'
Party,[25] an unregistered party counting 2,000 members,

> Turks and Albanians traditionally have good relations.
> There have been many mixed marriages. Our common
> religion is a very strong bond. ... Our traditionally good

---

[24] Human Rights Watch/Helsinki interview with Sezair Shaipi, head of the
Turkish Peoples' Party, in Prizren, December 1993.

[25] About ninety-five percent of the Turks in Kosovo participated in the
unofficial elections for the Republic of Kosovo. According to Mr. Shaipi, the goal
of his organization
> is to ensure equal rights for all national groups living in
> Kosovo. We want independence for Kosovo, but we never said
> whether it should be an independent state, or part of Serbia or
> Albania.
Human Rights Watch/Helsinki interview in Prizren, December 1993.

relations with the Serbs began to deteriorate after 1980, and especially between 1990 and 1993.

Now, however, Mr. Shaipi says that Turks are beset by a number of difficulties:

> Like Albanians, Turks are in a bad position before the Serbian regime.[26] This fact is concealed somewhat because it is hard to tell the difference between a Turkish and Albanian name. However, Albanians can speak their language in the courts, but we cannot speak Turkish.

Mr. Shaipi provided examples of several recent incidents of harassment of members of his organization and other Turks. For example, police recently detained Turan Fismis, the party's secretary, for forty-eight hours because he was caught with the party program, a public document that had been printed by the regular press. Mr. Shaipi said that last year he personally was attacked by police:

> At midnight on June 4, 1992, I was driving into Prizren with Sedat Morina, Afrim Morina and Marjan Spaqi. Our car stopped abruptly because of engine problems. Police shot at my car without cause or a warning. Sedat Morina lost an eye in the incident.

The policemen who had shot at them, Zoran Radovanović, Jozef Dekić and Zoran Stamenković, took the men to the police station for interrogation. Although Mr. Morina's wound needed immediate attention, the police wouldn't let him see a doctor. "We were detained for twenty-four hours and accused of an armed attack on the police patrol," Mr. Shaipi said. Mr. Shaipi and his colleagues pressed charges against the policemen, but as of this writing the court has yet to respond.

---

[26] Another Turkish man living in Kosovo disagreed with this statement, saying, "When the police come to my door, I still make sure they know I am Turkish, not Albanian." Human Rights Watch/Helsinki interview in Gnjilane, October 1993.

HARASSMENT OF TRADE UNIONS

In response to discrimination against non-Serbian employees in mid-1990, Albanians formed the Alliance of Independent Trade Unions of Kosovo (the Alliance). Today, the Alliance consists of twenty-two trade unions with over 260,000 members. They include more than 120,000 Albanians fired from their jobs by the regime in politically motivated purges since 1990. The Alliance, which provides its members legal advice and financial aid, survives on funds donated by Albanians working abroad and by various foreign humanitarian organizations.

The Alliance and its member unions are "under great pressure." According to Aziz Abrashi, the Vice President of the Alliance, members of the union "are harassed and threatened daily."[27]

In May 1993, police broke into the Alliance headquarters in Priština, seized documents and reportedly arrested and beat seven members. On October 2, 1993, the police again raided the Alliance offices and confiscated their computer, printer, typewriter and more documents.

Burhan Kavaja, the president of the Alliance's executive board, similarly recalled how he was beaten by four policemen in the street in Mitrovica on August 14, 1993:

When they identified me, they started beating me. They stole my watch and even tried to pull a wedding ring off my finger. They pulled until my finger started to bleed, but they had to give up. When they were through with me, I was covered in bruises, had torn earlobes and was severely depressed. I spent the next eighteen hours wrapped in ice.[28]

The latest such incident occurred on January 22, 1994. Adil Fetahu, the Alliance's general secretary, testified:

At 12:05 P.M., the police surrounded our building. Most were in plain clothes and some were in uniforms. They

---

[27] Human Rights Watch/Helsinki interview in Priština, January 1994.

[28] Human Rights Watch/Helsinki interview in Priština, January 1994.

were all armed. The police entered the building and
summoned about fifteen of our people into one room.
The rest of us were not allowed to leave. They checked
our IDs and released all but three of us.

Those men were members of the Independent Police
Union. They were detained for several hours, beaten
and released later that same day.[29]

DISRUPTION OF SPECIFIC EVENTS

In addition to targeting specific groups and individuals, Serbian
authorities have interfered with Albanian political meetings and local
party elections.[30] Moreover, according to the Council on Human Rights
and various LDK chapters, police interfere with Albanian cultural
gatherings with increasing frequency. One recent incident is described
below.

On August 13, 1993, at 5:30 P.M., police raided an Albanian
cultural celebration held at an elementary school[31] in Mitrovica. About
eighty Albanians had gathered there to celebrate the sixtieth anniversary
of the murder of an Albanian poet and patriot, Hasan Prishtina, who had
advocated democratic ideals. According to J.C., one of the participants,
about fifty heavily armed officers entered the school in a great display of
force:

When they came to the school, the policemen
demonstrated their force by playing with their machine
guns. They would cock them and point them at us. One
of them forced me to take down the [Albanian] national
flag that they had in the room. ... One interesting thing
is that among the people in the school there were old
people and religious leaders and intellectuals. The only

---

[29] Human Rights Watch/Helsinki interview in Priština, January 1994.

[30] For an account of interference with elections, see Helsinki Watch,
Yugoslavia: Human Rights Abuses in Kosovo: 1990-1992, October 1992, p. 20.

[31] The school was named "Migjeni."

guilt of these people was that they were present in a
cultural meeting of Albanians.[32]

Police arrested thirty-seven people out of the group and brought
them to the police station. One writer, J.C., described what happened to
him once he arrived at the station:

> When we arrived in front of the station, we saw police
> lined up in two lines. They forced us to run a gauntlet;
> the police beat us from all sides. Once inside the police
> station, they put us all in one room. Then they would
> pull us out of the room in two's and three's and beat us.
> We were all beaten from five to fifteen minutes.

Another man who had been taken to the station added:

> Once we were separated into two's and three's, they
> would force us to undress and they would joke among
> themselves about us. They tried to humiliate us. First
> they would beat us and then they would interrogate us.
> One question was "Why do you organize these kinds of
> meetings without permission of the police station? Why
> don't you accept the state of Serbia?" I said, "Because we
> have our own state." They kept us there from 5 P.M.
> until 11 P.M.. They warned us, "You will learn that this
> is Serbia, not Kosovo."[33]

The police singled out three men for special treatment,
apparently because they were suspected leaders. J.C. explained:

> In my case, I was kept at the police station for about two
> hours, then the police brought me back to my house. ...
> About twenty of them searched my house. I'm a

---

[32] Human Rights Watch/Helsinki interview in Mitrovica, September 1993.
Name withheld to protect witness.

[33] Human Rights Watch/Helsinki interview in Mitrovica, September 1993.
Name withheld to protect witness.

Professor of Literature so I have a lot of books. The first thing they said when they got inside my house was "Where do you work? What do you read? Where are your weapons?" My family was not at home. My bedroom door was closed and they broke the door down. After that, two policemen beat me with their fists on my head. Meanwhile, the others raided the house. They took my typewriter and some books. Then they put my personal documents back into my hands and brought me back to the police station. In all, they were in my house about forty minutes.[34]

Back at the police station, the abuse continued.

They brought me back to the third floor of the state security branch of the police. There were two inspectors in civilian clothes and two policemen in uniform. Two of them stayed with me all of the time and the other two went in and out. One of them opened the door and said, "Oh what a beast we have in here." They interrogated me here.

The police then brought J.C. into another room on the second floor of the station. There, they terrorized him so much, J.C. said, that he began to fear for his life.

One of the police said, "Shall we cut him into pieces?" During this time, one of them took a blanket and put it over my head. They started beating me again on the head. They would joke among themselves, asking me, "Who beats you now? Which of us now?" They started to say to each other, ironically, "You beat him up! No, you did! Don't beat him up, he's a professor."

After a short time, the police pulled the blanket off his head and all but one officer left the room.

---

[34] Human Rights Watch/Helsinki interview in Mitrovica, September 1993. Name withheld to protect witness.

The police officer left in the room started to interrogate
me again. He asked me, "Why don't you say that you
organized this?" During this time, one police officer
looked inside and then left the door open. This guy
stood outside the open door and began reading some of
the material he had taken from my house...Finally,
another inspector in civilian clothes came into the room
and said, "You can go home now, but you must come
back on Monday to get your stuff back." I went to the
station on Monday and two or three times after that and
they said, "What do you want! You are the enemy of the
Serbian people and you want us to give you your stuff
back!"

Police raided two other houses in a similar manner in connection
with the arrests at the school. Police took papers and books from all
houses and from one they confiscated a video camera.

The Albanians who weren't arrested didn't fare much better.
Instead of beating them in the police station, police simply beat them at
the school. As one man remembered:

They beat us with sticks and fists. They said, "If you
want next time to come into this school, you must take
your weapons with you. Why don't you start a war in
Kosovo?" They beat us for about an hour. The police
also lined both sides of the corridor of the school. To go
outside, you had to pass through the corridor; the police
on both sides beat you.

A doctor who treated many of those arrested stated that two of the men
had broken ribs; all had huge bruises.[35]

---

[35] Human Rights Watch/Helsinki interview in Mitrovica, September 1993.
Name withheld to protect witness.

MANIPULATION OF THE LEGAL SYSTEM
AND THE RIGHT TO A FAIR TRIAL

OVERVIEW OF THE FAILURES OF THE LEGAL SYSTEM

Through both law[1] and practice, Serbian authorities have taken over the judiciary in Kosovo. Several low-level courts and district attorney offices have been suspended, and the operations of judicial institutions have been turned over to Serbian hands.

By the fall of 1993, the vast majority of the Albanian judges and district attorneys had been dismissed and replaced with Serbs. The only Albanians remaining on the bench are so-called "honest Albanians" — Albanians who toe the Serbian line. According to Albanian defense attorneys, these Albanian judges are even more likely to be predisposed against Albanians than their Serbian counterparts.

Under such circumstances, few attorneys in Kosovo even speak of the independence of the judiciary any more. Defense attorneys lament that they no longer believe that their clients' innocence will save them — only a change of heart by the prosecuting official will do. In many cases reported by defense attorneys, investigations are carried out by the state security and the police rather than the prosecuting attorney, in violation of law, and administrative courts are used to pass judgments without any trial whatsoever.

In August-November 1993, Serbian police arrested several dozen Albanians, largely activists, men with former military experience and former political prisoners. Many cases were mass arrests, including more than a dozen people charged with related offenses.[2] The charges against

---

[1] Previously, Kosovo was an autonomous province in Serbia. The laws dissolving the former legal system which had given more independence to Albanians include: The Law on Changing and Complementing the Law on Judicial Courts and the Law on Changing and Complementing the Law on District Attorneys, *Official Gazette of Serbia*, No. 21/90; the Serbian Law on District Attorneys, *Official Gazette of Serbia*, No. 43/91; and the Serbian Law on the Judicial Courts, *Official Gazette of Serbia*, No. 46/91.

[2] The U.S. Department of State's 1993 Country Reports on Human Rights report similarly notes dozens of arrests in late 1993.

Albanians usually include allegations of "jeopardizing the territorial integrity of Yugoslavia"[3] — i.e. attempting to sever Kosovo from Serbia. To the extent that the sole reason for detention and imprisonment is actually non-violent association and expression of political views, these cases raise serious questions of violations of Articles 19 and 21 of the International Covenant of Civil and Political Rights (ICCPR), which, among other human rights instruments, grant all people the right to free speech and association.

As noted in the section on torture (see above), state security officers during interrogations routinely physically abuse their prisoners in order to exact confessions. The inability to do anything about torture of prisoners has led to a sense of futility among many Albanian lawyers. One of them, Destan Rukiqi, echoed the sentiments of many in stating:

> It is the same old thing. Yesterday, when I saw my client, he said to me, "They are beating me terribly. I don't know what they want from me." And he started crying. ... I was shocked by his condition. I am his defense attorney but there is nothing I can do to help him.[4]

Despite repeated objections of defense attorneys towards the abuse of detainees, courts in Kosovo refuse to take action against the police and members of the state security inflicting the torture. For instance, when defense attorneys for Ismet Mahmuti and Faik Ajeti objected to the police's attempt to torture their clients into confessing, the court simply replied that it "is not responsible for the actions of the

---

[3] Article 116, para. 1 of the Criminal Code of Yugoslavia. The courts in Serbia still use the old Law on Criminal Procedure adopted by the Socialist Federal Republic of Yugoslavia (SFRY) in 1976 and amended several times thereafter. The irony in charging people with "violating the territorial integrity of the SFRY" is evident — four of the six republics of the SFRY — Slovenia, Bosnia-Hercegovina, Croatia and Macedonia — are now recognized as independent states.

[4] Human Rights Watch/Helsinki interview in Priština, October 1993.

policemen."[5] When questioned by Human Rights Watch/Helsinki, the head of the District Court in Kosovo, Vojislav Živić, did not deny that Albanian prisoners are routinely beaten. On the contrary, he said that all of those beaten deserve it because they are threatening the territorial integrity of Yugoslavia. He stated, "When someone is accused of violating the territorial integrity of Yugoslavia, we can beat them and even kill them." When asked whether the beating could occur before trial, he quickly answered, "Yes." When then asked whether such a practice violates the principle that a person is innocent until proven guilty, he replied with a laugh, "But they can always appeal."[6]

In addition to the torture and cruel, inhuman and degrading treatment in detention, which in itself is a violation of international human rights instruments,[7] trials of Albanians are marked with a myriad of additional violations of the rights of the accused. These violations include the denial of the rights of the person arrested or detained to:

---

[5] See *A Response to the Complaint Against the Investigative Judge Dobrica Lazić and the Police Torture of the Accused*, September 2, 1993, Priština. For the allegations of torture in the case, see *Appeal on the Irregularities in the Court Procedure*, August 19, 1993, Priština; *Request for Medical Examination*, August 19, 1993 (defense attorney Bajram Kelmendi swearing that Ismet Mahmuti and Faik Ajeti "have informed me, and I was able to see for myself, that the police used force against them in an attempt to extract confessions. Visible wounds have been inflicted on them all over their bodies.") For similar allegations of torture in the case of Xhavit Haziri, see *Request for Medical Examination*, August 7, 1993; *Complaint Against Torture*, August 18, 1993, Priština (defense attorney Metush Sadiku swearing that "The accused Xhevad Hazari stated in front of the investigative judge on August 7, 1993, that he was tortured while in police custody. ... After the hearing on August 7, he was taken again to the police custody, tortured and interrogated until August 10. On August 16, the police used electric clubs on him which left visible marks on his body.").

[6] Human Rights Watch/Helsinki interview in Priština, October, 1993. When Mr. Živić was reminded that people cannot appeal after they're dead, he said, "But their families can appeal."

[7] See, *e.g.*, Article 7 of the International Covenant on Civil and Political Rights (hereafter ICCPR).

- Information upon arrest of the grounds for the arrest and any charges against him/her;[8]

- A prompt appearance brought before a judge or other officer authorized by law to exercise judicial power;[9]

- The right to initiate proceedings before a court so that the court may decide without delay on the lawfulness of the detention and order release if detention is not warranted;[10]

- Counsel of his/her own choosing;[11]

- Adequate time and facilities for the preparation of a defense and the ability to communicate with counsel;[12]

- A fair and open public hearing by a competent, independent tribunal;[13]

---

[8] ICCPR, Article 9(2).

[9] ICCPR, Article 9(3). Nearly all of the Albanians arrested recently are kept in custody for longer than three days without appearing before an investigative judge. According to Article 196 of the Federal Law on Criminal Procedure, the police can issue a detention warrant only in cases when there are grounds to believe that the suspect will destroy evidence. Such a detention can last no longer than three days, starting from the date of arrest.

The authorities regularly take advantage of Article 192, para. 3 of the Federal Law on Criminal Procedure, according to which detention warrants should be issued immediately or, at the latest, twenty-four hours after the arrest. By issuing the warrants twenty-four hours after the arrest, police ensure that detentions last a minimum of four days, instead of three.

[10] ICCPR, Article 9(4).

[11] ICCPR, Article 14(3)(b).

[12] ICCPR, Article 14(3)(b).

[13] ICCPR, Article 14(1).

- Equal treatment before courts and tribunals;[14]

- A presumption of innocence until proven guilty by law;[15]

- Trial without unreasonable delay;[16]

- Trial in his/her own presence, and the right to defend himself/herself in person or through legal assistance of his/her own choosing;[17]

- Examination of the witnesses against him/her and the right to obtain the attendance and examination of witnesses on his/her behalf under the same condition as witnesses against him/her;[18]

- The ability to remain silent at trial and not be compelled to testify against himself/herself or to confess guilt;[19]

- If convicted, the right to have the sentence reviewed by a higher tribunal that is also competent and impartial and established according to law;[20] and

---

[14] ICCPR, Article 14(1).

[15] ICCPR, Article 14(2).

[16] ICCPR, Article 9(3) and 14(3)(c).

[17] ICCPR, Article 14(3)(d).

[18] ICCPR, Article 14(3)(e).

[19] ICCPR, Article 14(3)(g).

[20] ICCPR, Article 14(5).

•   Compensation for unlawful arrest or detention.[21]

By highlighting the denial of these guarantees, the following recent cases, although just a fraction of the recent explosion of arrests, serve to exemplify the extent to which the Serb-dominated legal system denies Albanians these basic rights.

CASES EXEMPLIFYING DUE PROCESS VIOLATIONS[22]

The 1992 Trial and Appeal of 19 Albanians for Anti-Serbian Activities

On October 11, 1993, the Supreme Court of Serbia heard the appeal of nineteen men who had been found guilty a year earlier of having founded an illegal organization and conspired to purchase weapons to advance secessionist aims.[23] The lower court had sentenced the men to between one-to-three and four-to-seven years. As of this writing—over four months after the appeal was heard—the Supreme Court has not yet ruled on the case, in violation of Yugoslav law which provides for speedy verdicts. This case, as detailed below, illustrates well the type of abuses rampant in the criminal justice system.

---

[21] ICCPR, Article 9(5). See also Article 14(6)(grounds for post-conviction compensation upon the discovery of a new fact that shows conclusively that there has been a miscarriage of justice).

[22] For some cases prior to 1993, see Helsinki Watch, *Yugoslavia: Human Rights Abuses in Kosovo 1990-1992*, October 1992, pp. 22-28.

[23] Human Rights Watch/Helsinki representatives attended the hearing on the appeal in Priština on October 11, 1993. The following information, unless otherwise noted, is drawn from the arguments made at that hearing and court submissions and decisions (all a matter of public record and also on file with Human Rights Watch/Helsinki). Eight other ethnic Albanians accused of similar offenses were tried in the District Court of Priština in October 1992. See Amnesty International, Kosovo Concerns, EUR/70/01/93, February 2, 1993.

The Charges

The charges against each of the accused are as follows:[24]

1. Mentor Kaqi (born in 1952), goldsmith, father of three —
Accused of "set[ting] up an illegal enemy organization "National
Front of Albanians," coordinat[ing] with military experts abroad
(Austria, Switzerland, Albania), and at home with a goal to
separate Kosovo from Serbia and Yugoslavia...; [Visiting]
Switzerland and Albania [to raise] money for the organization...;
[Acquiring] three machine guns, four revolvers, one pistol, one
semi-automatic gun and five hand grenades as well as
ammunition from an unidentified person in Switzerland..."

2. Sokol Dobruna (born in 1940), lawyer, father of three —
Accused of "help[ing] set up an illegal enemy organization
"National Front of Albanians"; search[ing] for military experts,
mainly Albanian reserve officers...; Travel[ing] to Croatia,
Switzerland and Albania [to] raise money for the organization..."

3. Naim Krasniqi (born in 1953), unemployed, father of three —
Accused of "lobby[ing] for forceful separation of Kosovo from
Serbia and Yugoslavia; [being] in charge of the military aspect of
the organization; visit[ing] Albania and Greece and
reconnoiter[ing] the Albanian-Yugoslav border in order to find
the most convenient crossing points;"

4. Fatlik Lila (born in 1951), married, father of four — Accused of
having helped set up and organize the National Front of
Albanians;

5. Afrim Morina (born in 1951), teacher and former political
prisoner, father of three — Accused of helping set up and
organize an illegal enemy organization and purchasing arms in
Greece;

---

[24] This listing is drawn from *The Indictment of 19 Persons for the Foundation of
the National Albanian Front and their Activities,* March 25, 1992 (filed in Peć).

6. Qerkin Peci (born in 1944), former political prisoner, retired, father of three — Accused of helping set up an illegal organization;

7. Sejdi Veseli (born in 1949), former political prisoner, unemployed — Accused of being a member of the presidency of the National Front of Albanians and having helped set up an illegal organization;

8. Deli Haxhocaj (born in 1957), completed course requirements for medical school, father of three — Accused of having joined the National Front of Albanians in 1991 and being in charge of health care plan for war situations;

9. Sadik Mulaj (born in 1957), unemployed mechanical engineer, former political prisoner, father of four — Accused of being a member of the National Front of Albanians and illegally acquiring guns and ammunition;

10. Zenel Sadiku (born in 1948), unemployed teacher, father of four, former political prisoner — Accused of being a member of the National Front of Albanians and being in charge of the illegal crossing at the Albanian-Yugoslav border;

11. Palush Palushaj (born in 1960), father of one child — Accused of being active in the Djakovica branch of the National Front of Albanians;

12. Gëzim Efendija (born in 1949), employed with the Djakovica municipality, father of two — Accused of having helped set up a National Front of Albanians chapter for military activities;

13. Selajdin Doli (born in 1956), graduated from the school of national defense, employed with the Serbian ministry of defense, regional office in Djakovica — Accused of compiling a list of Albanian defense officers and of non-Albanian officers who would be disarmed at the appropriate time;

14. Nazim Këpuska (born in 1938), manual worker — Accused of helping set up the Djakovica chapter of the organization and of allowing his house to be used for meetings;

15. Shukri Zërza (born in 1943), employed with the Serbian ministry of defense, father of two — Accused of having helped set up the Djakovica chapter and organizing the purchase of walkie-talkies;

16. Salih Caka (born in 1944), sales person, father of three — Accusing of having helped set up the Djakovica chapter and of being in charge of plumbing in case of war;

17. Nuhi Bytyqi (born in 1954), economist, father of two, former political prisoner — Accused of allowing gatherings of members of the organization in his shop and serving as a messenger for the organization;

18. Sali Dahsuli (born in 1953), worker, father of five — Accused of stealing canvas for military uniforms for the National Front of Albanians from "Napredak," a textile factory in Djakovica; and

19. Mehdi Hasi (born in 1956), mechanic, father of two — Accused of taking part in military exercises for the National Front of Albanians.

The Procedural Defects

The appeal in this case centered on the numerous procedural defects in the original trial and the grossly abusive treatment of the accused, in violation of both federal and international law.[25] According to Bajram Kelmendi, one of the lawyers for two of the men:

> From the very beginning, the defense was cut out, which means we were not allowed to look through any documentation throughout the investigation. They didn't let us see anything — any evidence against them, exculpatory evidence, doctors reports, etc. — until they pressed charges. Also, the investigation was not carried out by the investigative judge who should have done this according to law. Instead, the investigation was done by the members of the state security.[26]

---

[25] Along with the various defects listed below, the defense attorneys argued that the prosecution and the defense are acting according to the laws of a country that no longer exists, that the allegations in the indictment were vague, contradictory, and not supported by sufficient evidence, and that the sentences were too severe for the acts for which the accused had been charged. See *Appeal to the Supreme Court of Serbia, Belgrade, through the District Court of Peć, on the Sentence of the District Court of Peć on October 20, 1992, By the Defense Attorney of the Accused Sokol Dobruna and Gëzim Efendija*, December 25, 1992, Priština.

[26] Human Rights Watch/Helsinki interview in Priština, October 1993.

Mr. Kelmendi submitted a complaint alleging that the defense attorneys had been denied access to relevant court documents;[27] the court promptly rejected his claims.

The court permitted the families of the accused to be present at the trial but not the prisoners themselves.[28] There were no witnesses in the trial by either side. Instead, the evidence consisted of the statements of the accused. The accused gave statements on two occasions. According to Mr. Kelmendi,

> The first time the accused gave statements to the investigative judge, there was not enough information for the judge to press charges. So he turned the case back over to the secret police.[29] ... The police again

---

[27] *Complaint of Defense Attorney*, dated December 27, 1991 (submitted to the President of the Peć) district court). Article 73 of the Yugoslav Law on Criminal Procedure provides as follows:
   Par. 1: A defense attorney is allowed access to court documents and material evidence after an investigation warrant is issued or an indictment is handed down. A defense attorney is entitled to have access to court records if a client has been interrogated in the role of the accused.
   Par. 2: In certain circumstances where the security of the country may be in jeopardy, prior to the indictment, the defense attorney can be banned from reviewing court material and evidence.
   Par. 3: It is possible to appeal a decision from Par. 2 to the court council but this does not hinder the implementation of the decision from Par. 2.
Translation of this law, and all laws noted in this report have been carried out by Human Rights Watch/Helsinki.

[28] Article 281 of the Yugoslav Law on Criminal Procedure states that the accused must be invited to the trial.

[29] Article 161 of the Yugoslav Law on Criminal Procedure provides:
   Par. 1: The investigation is to be carried out by the investigative judge of the competent court.

questioned the accused, although they had already given
their statements. No lawyers were present. They used
torture. And the statements they gave were diametrically
opposed to the statements they gave earlier due to this
torture.

According to the lawyers representing the accused, the men had
been beaten before they gave their second confessions. Indeed, the
family members of several of the men as well as their lawyers told
Human Rights Watch/Helsinki of visiting the accused in prison and being
startled by their bruised and broken condition. For example, X.S. told
Human Rights Watch/Helsinki that when he visited one of the arrested
men (his cousin) in prison, he was in very bad condition. "When I first
saw him, he had been beaten so badly that he couldn't life his arms," X.S.
recalled, adding "They had also pulled out his hair."[30] Prison medical
reports specifically include evidence of wounds inflicted while the men
were in prison.

Not only do the prison beatings violate the rights of the accused
not to be tortured,[31] the defense attorneys argued, such treatment

-----

However, according to Article 162, par. 4 of the same law, the
investigative judge can, at the public prosecutor's suggestion and after a proper
finding, turn over the investigation to the police if the case involves a suspected
threat to national security. If the investigative judge disapproves of the
prosecutor's suggestion, he must seek the court council's opinion, which in turn
must render a final decision within twenty four hours.

[30] Human Rights Watch/Helsinki interview in Peć, October 1993. Identity of
person withheld for protection.

[31] Article 65 of the Criminal Code of Serbia and Article 190 of the Yugoslav
Criminal Code provide as follows:
     Par 1: An official who uses force, threat or other
     illegal methods in the line of duty or attempts in any other
     prohibited way to extract a statement from the accused or a
     witness shall be punished for between three months to five
     years in prison.
     Par. 2: If the confession was extracted under torture,
     or if the extracted confession worsened the accused's position
     at trial, the perpetrator will be sentenced to at least one year.

violates the accused's right to be silent and not testify against himself.[32] At the trial and on appeal, the defense team suggested that the second set of statements given by the accused be stricken from the record because they were given only after the police used force. "It is enough to compare the statements of the accused in front of the investigative judge and those in front of the police — they are different," Mr. Kelmendi argued, "and they show the result of the police torture upon the accused."[33] Still, despite the evidence of mistreatment of the prisoners, both on trial and on appeal, the courts rejected this argument.

The defense attorneys also protested that the authorities had withheld information about the charges and that their clients had been held without the right to any counsel for two months.[34] Once the defense lawyers were allowed to see their clients, they could not speak freely with them in a confidential setting. Mr. Kelmendi, voicing the concerns of many other defense lawyers in the case, explained that:

> during the discussions with the accused, they did not let us talk about their criminal acts as the law allows so we could prepare a defense. ... A state security officer was posted nearby during our talks to make sure that we didn't talk about the subject. We could only ask them if they needed anything, etc. How could we prepare a defense![35]

---

[32] Article 218 of the Yugoslav Law on Criminal Procedure.

[33] *The Final Word of Defense Attorney Bajram Kelmendi*, October 16, 1992, Priština.

[34] A sworn statement of Mr. Kelmendi, requesting permission to see one of his clients, states that "On December 27, 1991, I requested to see the accused Sokol Dobruna, but was denied the permit by the investigative judge, although he had no legal grounds to do so." *A Request for the Permission of Lawyer Bajram Kelmendi to See the Accused Dobruna, Sokol,* dated December 27, 1991 (submitted to the investigative judge of the Peć District Court) (translated from Serbian).

[35] Human Rights Watch/Helsinki interview in Priština, October 1993.

This practice is in direct violation the Federal Law on Criminal Procedure.[36] Mr. Kelmendi and other defense attorneys submitted complaints about these procedural defects to the president of the court. The court flatly rejected the complaints, stating that it had no jurisdiction to act on them, and that such issues should be brought instead to the Supreme Court of Serbia. The Supreme Court of Serbia, however, responded that it could not consider the procedural defects until the case was over.

The defense lawyers also submitted papers demanding that the President of the Court Council and various other judges and the Republic Public Prosecutor be disqualified from the case.[37] The papers suggested that the President should be excluded because he had done nothing after the lawyers had complained about irregularities with the investigative procedure, including the inability of defense counsel to speak freely with the accused, and the use of force to produce confessions. At the same time, the lawyers argued that the Prosecutor should be excused because he did not write the accusations against the defendants, as required by law, but instead allowed the accusations to be written by a Deputy Prosecutor sent in for the case from Belgrade. The court rejected these claims as well, ruling that the request for disqualification of the judges

---

[36] Article 74 of the Yugoslav Law on Criminal Procedure provides:

Par. 1: A defense attorney is allowed to talk to and exchange letters with his detained client after he has been interrogated.

Par. 2: An investigative judge can decide to read letters from the accused to the defense attorney and vice versa prior to delivery, or to deny the attorney the right to private conversations with his client.

Par. 3: Once the interrogation is completed, or the indictment is handed down, the accused cannot be denied the right to freely and without supervision exchange letters and talk to his defense attorney.

[37] *The Request for the Disqualification of the President of the Court Council Živojin Cvjetić*, May 11, 1993, Peć.

was "unfounded"[38] and that the request for removal of the Public Prosecutor was a question for the Federal Public Prosecutor.[39]

This set of rulings resulted in an absurd situation, Mr. Kelmendi explained:

> because the defense attorneys sought to excuse the Federal Prosecutor from the case as well, they couldn't appeal to the Federal Prosecutor. Instead, the Deputy Prosecutor had to decide the case. In other words, the Deputy had to decide for his boss. ... We sent another complaint about this situation to the Deputy and of course he rejected it. We wanted the Supreme Court of Serbia to decide the question, but the President of the District Court threatened us when we tried to do this, saying "I'll use different methods with you!" So the trial just continued and no one was excused, despite their demonstrated prejudice against us.

The conduct of the Serb authorities in connection with this case, and the numerous procedural defects, not the least of which is the compelling evidence of forced confessions, raise grave concerns about the impartiality of the justice system.

The 1993 Case Against Five Men in Prizren

On August 2-4, 1993, the Prizren police arrested ten ethnic Albanian men in a single sweep. After police interrogated all of the men, they released five of them. At hearings on August 12, 1993, investigative judge Nikola Vazura found that there was cause to hold the remaining five men for another 30 days and to start a formal investigation against them. On September 18, District Public Prosecutor Dobrovoje Perić

---

[38] *The Rejection of the Request for the Disqualification of the Judge Časlav Ignjatović and President of Council of the District Court in Peć, Živojin Cvjetić, as requested by Kaci Mentor*, July 5, 1992, Peć.

[39] *The Proposal By the Defense Attorneys for the Request for the Protection of Law in the Case of the Disqualification of the Republic Public Prosecutor of Serbia*, July 10, 1992, Peć.

indicted the five for alleged involvement in an illegal organization called the National Movement for the Republic of Kosovo (NPRK).

The trial of all five men — Behajdin Allaqi (age thirty), Ilaz Kadolli (age forty-four), Hysen Gegaj (age forty-four), Binak Berisha (age thirty-one) and Shefki Muqaj (age fifty) — was held on November 2-11, 1993,[40] before Judge Nada Nadži-Perić of the Prizren District Court.

A Human Rights Watch/Helsinki representative monitored the conclusion of the trial on November 10-11. Although permission was given by the presiding judge to be present at the trial (which, in any event, was an open proceeding), the Human Rights Watch/Helsinki representative was detained and interrogated immediately after the trial ended. In front of the courthouse, three police officers armed with machine guns approached the Human Rights Watch/Helsinki researcher and a British television journalist and ordered them to get into their car. They took them both to the Prizren police station.

The police interrogated the Human Rights Watch/Helsinki representative for four hours before, bowing to pressure from foreign journalists and the U.S. embassy, they eventually released the representative. The police interrogated the British journalist about her contacts as well, and confiscated the material that she had filmed with the court president's permission. (For a full account of this incident, see above).

The Human Rights Watch/Helsinki representative was present when the judge convicted all of the men under Article 136, Paragraph 2, to Article 116 of the Criminal Code of Yugoslavia, prohibiting membership in a group intended to commit enemy activities against

---

[40] On November 2, the lawyers for the first four of the accused gave their defenses; on November 3, the lawyer for Muqaj gave his; on November 10, the prison doctor read the medical reports and the accused gave their closing arguments, and on November 11, the judge pronounced the sentence.

Yugoslavia.[41] Each man's case illustrates due process violations and thus is summarized briefly below.

Behajdin Allaqi

Mr. Allaqi, father of two and a teacher of philosophy, is a member of the Prizren chapter of the Democratic League of Kosova (LDK). He was arrested off the street in Prizren on August 1, 1993. The police searched his house later that evening and found the program and statue of the National Movement for the Republic of Kosovo (NPRK), a purported Albanian separatist party, as well as a pistol that belonged to his father.[42]

Mr. Allaqi was interrogated about his political activities by the police for two days before he received a detention warrant, in apparent violation of the law which states that such warrants must be issued within twenty four hours.[43] Also in apparent violation of the law,[44] his lawyers saw him for the first time eleven days after his arrest, when he appeared at an August 12th hearing before investigative judge Nikola Vazura. There, Mr. Allaqi stated that his confession was extracted under

---

[41] Article 136 of the Yugoslav Criminal Code, Para. 1, provides:

Whoever forms a conspiracy, gang, group or some other association of citizens in order to commit felonies as specified in [listing several articles pertaining to anti-Yugoslav activities] ..., or whoever forms a group with the intention to send Yugoslav citizens abroad in order to carry out enemy activities against Yugoslavia, will be sentenced up to five years.

Paragraph 2 of the same article further specifies that "Whoever becomes a member of an association as specified in para. 1 of this article will be sentenced to at least one year in prison."

[42] At a separate court processing before the Prizren Municipal Court, Mr. Allaqi was sentenced to three months for unlawful possession of a weapon.

[43] The Yugoslav Law on Criminal Procedure (Article 192, para. 3) allows a maximum twenty-four hours detention at the police station without a detention warrant. An investigative judge of the court issues such warrants.

[44] Article 67, para. 1 of the Yugoslav Law on Criminal Procedure specifies that "the accused has the right to a lawyer throughout all criminal proceedings."

torture.[45] According to Mr. Allaqi, police beat him severely all over his body, feet and hands. A report by a prison doctor who examined Allaqi indeed confirmed that he was bruised on his arms and lower back.[46]

After the hearing before the investigative judge, Mr. Allaqi was taken back to the state security officers for further interrogation. Yet, the judge had not turned the investigation over to the police; nor had he granted written permission for this set of interrogations. These latter interrogation sessions thus violate the Yugoslav Law on Criminal Procedure which, absent specific written permission of the judge, prohibits police interrogations of suspects after the hearing before the investigative judge.[47]

Mr. Allaqi's family was allowed to visit him in prison for the first time on August 17, more than two weeks after his arrest. According to family members, he was under tranquilizers and appeared cowed. He told them that he was urinating blood.[48]

On September 18, 1993, Mr. Allaqi was indicted for joining the NPRK in Switzerland in 1987. The District Public Prosecutor further stated that Mr. Allaqi adopted the pseudonym of "Besim" and had accepted the NPRK program calling for the secession of Kosovo by force from rump Yugoslavia.

At the hearings before the Prizren District Court, Mr. Allaqi and his lawyers denied that he is a member of any other political party but the LDK. They insisted that, being a political scientist, he collected

---

[45] Article 218, Para. 8 of the Yugoslav Law on Criminal Procedure reads as follows:

> Force, threat or any similar measures cannot
> be applied in order to obtain the accused's
> statement or extract his confession.

[46] The doctor read the medical reports in open court on November 10, 1993.

[47] Article 162, Para. 4, of the Yugoslav Law on Criminal Procedure allows police interrogations of the suspect after the hearing by the investigative judge only with the investigative judge's written permission, issued at the prosecutor's request.

[48] Human Rights Watch/Helsinki interview with family members in Priština, November 1993.

programs of all parties and movements existing in Serbia and former Yugoslavia and that the fact that he had a program of the NPRK does not imply that he adopted it. Mr. Allaqi explained that he was working in Switzerland illegally and that he used a pseudonym to disguise his real identity because of frequent controls by the Swiss police.

The judge rejected Mr. Allaqi's defense and found him guilty on November 11, 1993, sentencing him to two years in prison.[49]

Ilaz Kadolli

Mr. Kadolli, a lawyer and father of three, was arrested on the street in Prizren on the morning of August 2, 1993. The police denied to his family and legal counsel that they were holding him until August 6, 1993. On that day, his lawyer, Hysni Bytyqi, saw him for the first time. Mr. Bytyqi remembered:

> I was told [by Mr. Kadolli] that they [Mr. Kadolli and Hysen Gegaj] were held at the police station all this time. Both were constantly interrogated and beaten while tied to radiators throughout the first ninety six hours of detention. [Mr. Kadolli] told me that they untied his hands only when they were beating him and that he was prepared to confess to anything only if they would stop.[50]

Mr. Bytyqi was shocked by his client's condition. According to Mr. Bytyqi, "his face and hands were swollen and all exposed parts of his body were bruised."[51]

The prison doctor confirmed Mr. Bytyqi's assessment. His official report found bruises on his arms, legs and lower back that were "most probably inflicted by a blunt object."[52] During a search of Mr.

---

[49] His lawyers were Engjell Çeta, Ruzhdi Berisha, and Fatmir Celina.

[50] Human Rights Watch/Helsinki interview in Prizren, November 1993.

[51] *Id.*

[52] The doctor read the medical reports in open court on November 10, 1993.

Kadolli's home, the police found one semi-automatic rifle.[53]   However, the police recovered no other physical evidence against Mr. Kadolli.

At his trial before the Prizren District Court on November 2, 1993, Mr. Kadolli insisted that he is only a LDK member, and that he has never been a member of the NPRK. According to Mr. Kadolli, the first time he even saw the program for the NPRK was in the police station upon his arrest.

Mr. Kadolli alleged that two policemen who said that they were with Arkan's Tigers, an infamous paramilitary group,[54] beat him in the police station. He testified that police tied him to a radiator and beat him continually for the first four days of his detention.

As with the other prisoners, the court summarily rejected Mr. Kadolli's defense and sentenced him to two-and-a-half-years in prison.

Hysen Gegaj

Mr. Gegaj, a carpenter and father of four, formerly served a twelve-year sentence as a political prisoner. He was arrested at his house on the morning of August 2, 1993. Like Mr. Kadolli, police interrogated and tortured him at the police station for four days before his family was informed of his whereabouts.

On August 6, police took Mr. Gegaj to a hearing in front of an investigative judge. This was the first time Mr. Gegaj saw his lawyer, Hysny Bytyqi. Mr. Bytyqi was shaken by the sight of his client:

> He could barely walk. He had to keep his legs apart.
> His face and all exposed parts of his body were covered
> with bruises. The policemen did not allow him to take

---

[53] In a separate procedure, the Municipal Court sentenced him to fourteen months in prison for unlawful possession of a weapon.

[54] Arkan is the *nom de guerre* of Željko Ražnjatović, a reputed organized crime boss with close ties to the Milošević regime. He is also the commander of the Serbian Tigers, a notorious paramilitary unit suspected of committing war crimes in Croatia and Bosnia-Hercegovina.

his shirt off to show me the bruises on the rest of his body. I cried when I saw what they had done to him.[55]

Police threatened Mr. Gegaj to confess "or else." Based on the document purporting to be the "confession" of the prisoner, the investigative judge ordered that there was cause to hold him for another thirty days.

The lawyer attempted in vain to report the abuse. "When I complained to the prison warden," Mr. Bytyqi said, "the police threatened to arrest me too."[56]

The police found a handgun and automatic rifle in Mr. Gegaj's house.[57] Mr. Gegaj was indicted for being a member of the NPRK since 1990, attending meetings and accepting the responsibility to organize the evacuation of the civilian population of his village in case of war. The indictment does not specify when or where the meetings in question were held, nor does it indicate what "accepting the responsibility" means.

At his hearing before the District Court, Mr. Gegaj testified that he was asked to join the NPRK, but he declined the invitation since he had already decided to join the LDK. According to Mr. Gegaj, he never attended any meetings of the NPRK. Asked why his statement before the court differed from that given to the investigative judge three months earlier, Mr. Gegaj said that he was beaten so badly by the police that he was prepared to sign a confession saying that it was he who dropped the atomic bomb on Hiroshima.[58]

On November 11, the court found Hysen Gegaj guilty and sentenced him to three and a half years in prison.

---

[55] Human Rights Watch/Helsinki interview in Prizren, November 1993.

[56] Id.

[57] In separate proceedings, the Prizren Municipal Court sentenced Mr. Gegaj to eleven months for unlawful possession of arms.

[58] From notes of a Human Rights Watch/Helsinki observer at trial in Prizren in November 1993.

Binak Berisha

Mr. Berisha, a physics teacher and father of one, is also a former political prisoner. Mr. Berisha was arrested on August 4, 1993, and interrogated about unlawful possession of arms. The indictment prepared against Mr. Berisha, however, does not mention arms, but rather accuses Mr. Berisha of joining the NPRK in 1979, recruiting new members and distributing party propaganda material. Berisha thus was never questioned about the crime he was eventually tried and sentenced for.

Mr. Berisha's lawyer, Hazër Susuri, saw him for the first time on August 20, 1993. Mr. Susuri told Human Rights Watch/Helsinki:

> [Mr. Berisha] told me that he was beaten repeatedly between August 4 and August 17. He was visibly exhausted. His feet were bruised and he could barely walk. Police had constantly interrogated and beaten him for five days while he was handcuffed to a steel cupboard in the police station.[59]

Like the other men, the investigative judge that found cause to hold Mr. Berisha did so on the basis on a "confession" the prisoner had signed after police had threatened to beat him to death. According to his lawyer, Mr. Berisha was summoned several times to the police station for further interrogation after he had been questioned by the investigative judge, in violation of the Federal Code of Criminal Procedure.

At his hearing on November 2nd, Mr. Berisha denied all accusations against him and stated firmly that he is a member of the LDK and of no other party. He testified that he was tortured at the police station and that the police officers who had beaten him advised him to testify against the other four accused. According to Mr. Berisha, the officers promised that they would provide him with a valid passport and allow him to flee the country in return for his testimony. Like the other men, Mr. Berisha attributed the difference between his November 2nd statement and his earlier statement to the investigative judge to the torture he had endured at the hand of the police and the fear that it

---

[59] Human Rights Watch/Helsinki interview in Prizren, November 1993.

would continue if he refused to confess to the specific charges they had already prepared against him.

On November 11, 1993, the court found Mr. Berisha guilty and sentenced him to three years in prison.

Shefki Muqaj

Mr. Muqaj, a teacher and father of four, served a four-year prison term in the early 1960s. He was arrested as the fifth defendant of the case against alleged members of the NPRK on August 7, 1993. Like the others, on the basis of a "confession" signed after police threatened to kill him, Mr. Muqaj was indicted for being a member of the NPRK and for attending meetings of the outlawed group.

At a Prizren District Court hearing on November 3, 1993, he denied membership in the NPRK, asserting that he is a member of the LDK. Mr. Muqaj also stated that his "confession" before the investigative judge on August 12, 1993, was a result of repeated beatings by the police while he was in detention. On November 11, 1993, the trial court found Mr. Muqaj guilty and sentenced him to three and a half years in prison.

December 1993 Trial of LDK Leader in Prizren

Ukë Bytyqi, a thirty-eight-year-old agricultural engineer from Suva Reka/Suharakë, the president of a local LDK chapter and father of three, was recently sentenced to five years on trumped up charges of "jeopardizing the territorial integrity of Yugoslavia."[60]

Mr. Bytyqi was arrested on October 5, 1993, at 1:00 P.M. at the LDK office in Suva Reka and taken to the police station in Prizren. At the station, he met Kadrija Balaj, another officer in the LDK chapter. Before letting Mr. Balaj go, police wrote down his name and promised to come back for him. Mr. Balaj fled abroad the same day. Hours later, police searched the LDK office and Mr. Bytyqi's house, but they did not find any evidence of his alleged illegal activities. The police confiscated a new computer belonging to the LDK that had not even been unpacked. The police then turned their attention back to Mr. Bytyqi.

At his trial on December 9, 1993, Mr. Bytyqi recalled:

---

[60] Article 116, para. 1 of the Criminal Code of Yugoslavia.

For the next forty-eight hours [after my arrest], I was
physically and psychologically tortured, without food,
water or a moment of sleep.   Ten state security
inspectors constantly interrogated and beat me. I was
either tied to a radiator or had my hands cuffed behind
my back. I asked for food and drink. But they refused
to give me anything before I signed a "confession" which
they wrote themselves. Several policemen at a time beat
me with truncheons over my entire body, feet and hands.
They repeatedly tried to hit me in the genitals.[61]

At 5:00 A.M. on October 6th, the police took Mr. Bytyqi to the
home of Kadrija Balaj in the village of Doberdolan. Kadrija's brother,
Raif Balaj, a forty-three-year-old farmer told Human Rights
Watch/Helsinki:

I woke up to the barking of dogs and saw five or six
machine guns pointed at me through the window. I
opened the door. Ukë was in the middle of several
policemen. As they were handcuffing me, they said, "You
see who brought us to your door!" Ukë looked terrible.
I noticed an open wound on the side of his neck. They
pushed him back into the car and hit him in front of us.
... After a search that lasted about two hours, they
ordered me and Jashar Balaj's father, Selim, to get into
the car with Ukë.[62]

Police interrogated Raif Balaj at the police station about his own and his
brother's political activities until about 5:00 P.M..
According to Mr. Bytyqi, the next day police forced him to sign
a confession:

On October 7th, two of those policemen took me to the
investigative judge. The policeman told me: "If you try

---

[61] From notes of Human Rights Watch/Helsinki observer at trial on December
9, 1993.

[62] Human Rights Watch/Helsinki interview in Prizren, December 1993.

to deny, or to change this statement, if you don't confess to everything, we will take you to the Albanian border at night, shoot you and say that you were killed in an attempt to escape." In order to save my life, I signed what I was told to.[63]

Two of the policemen who allegedly beat Mr. Bytyqi during his first two days in detention were present throughout the hearing in front of investigative judge Nikola Vazura. Mr. Vazura, who is also president of the Prizren District Court, denied Mr. Bytyqi's lawyer permission to be present at the first of the two hearings he held.

On October 19, the District Prosecutor, Dobrovoje Perić, indicted Mr. Bytyqi on charges of being a coordinator and commander of a covert ethnic Albanian military headquarters in his town. The indictment further accused Mr. Bytyqi of:

> along with Ibrahim Shala, Kadri Balaj, Zyba Myftar and Sulejman Sopaja, acting under Ram Maraj's instructions, preparing to use force to jeopardize the constitutional order and sever a part of Yugoslavia and a part of the Republic of Serbia — the territory of Kosovo and Metohija populated by ethnic Albanians, taking an active role in organizing paramilitary formations in Suva Reka, helping to set up eleven military units with about 2,400 people, appointing commanding officers, organizing support units and a communication system, forming a special unit that was to have about ten people, based on the lists of voters that were used for the illegal elections for the parliament of the republic of Kosovo, making lists of army reservists, commanding officers, draftees and plans for combat, and giving all of this material to Kadri Balaj who hid it with his cousin, Jashar Balaj.[64]

---

[63] From notes of Human Rights Watch/Helsinki observer at trial on December 9, 1993.

[64] From indictment of Ukë Bytyqi, dated October 19, 1993.

The indictment names no witnesses and lists no evidence other than "an Epson-570 computer that was *to be* used to commit a felony." (emphasis added)

A Human Rights Watch/Helsinki representative was present at Mr. Bytyqi's trial before the Prizren District Court judge Nada Hadži-Perić on December 9, 1993. Mr. Bytyqi and his defense attorneys, Hazër Susuri and Fazli Balaj, denied all charges and insisted that the police used torture to extract his "confession." Judge Hadži-Perić asked the prosecutor, Dobrovoje Perić, whether he would offer any witnesses or material evidence. He replied that he would not and referred her only to Mr. Bytyqi's statement given to the investigative judge two days after his arrest. One of the two members of the Court Council hearing the case, walked out while the defense attorneys were delivering their closing arguments, thus strengthening the belief that the final outcomes of the current rash of prosecutions of ethnic Albanians are decided beforehand.[65]

The next day, December 10, 1993, judge Hadži-Perić sentenced Mr. Bytyqi to five years in prison.

January 1994 Trial of Four Albanians in Peć

On October 1, 1991, a group of about fifty Albanians met in a house of Sadri Shala in the village of Dobra Voda/Ujëmirë, near Klina. Several were members of the National Movement for the Republic of Kosovo (NPRK). They dined and discussed the political situation in Kosovo.

Two years later, police arrested Fisnik Čukaj, Sadri Shala, Ymer Shala and Ali Lajci in connection with this meeting. For several days after arrest, local police repeatedly tortured the men. Subsequently, the four all signed "confessions" prepared by the police officers. Only after this point did the authorities allowed them to contact their lawyers. The accused were tried in the Peć District Court in January 1994. A Human Rights Watch/Helsinki representative monitored the trial.

---

[65] From notes of Human Rights Watch/Helsinki observer at trial on December 9, 1993.

Fisnik Čukaj

Fisnik Čukaj, twenty-six-year-old student from Peć, was arrested on August 31, 1993. Mr. Čukaj testified that he was tortured for four days in the police station. As a result, he "confessed" to being a member of the NPRK, recruiting his two best friends for the organization, and meeting with them on two occasions. One of the policemen who Mr. Čukaj claimed had beaten him was present at his September 3 hearing before an investigative judge, Dušan Mičanović. At this hearing, Mr. Čukaj confirmed his earlier "confession"; later, Mr. Čukaj alleged that he had felt threatened by the presence of his torturer.

His defense attorney, Adem Bajri, saw him for the first time at his second hearing before the investigative judge, on September 8.[66] At this point, Mr. Čukaj insisted that his confession had been extracted under torture. Mr. Bajri recalled:

> He had visible signs of torture on his face and all exposed parts of his body. During the visit [later that day], I saw that his entire body was covered with bruises — especially the feet, hands and the kidney area.[67]

The investigative judge issued a detention warrant on September 8.

Public Prosecutor Miladin Popović indicted Mr. Čukaj on November 23, on charges of attending the October 1, 1991 meeting "as a guest," joining the NPRK in late 1991, recruiting two other people for this organization and meeting with them on two occasions. Their actions, according to the prosecutor, constituted violations of Article 136, Para. 1 to Article 116, Paragraph 1 of the Criminal Code of Yugoslavia — forming

---

[66] The fact that Čukaj didn't have a lawyer for the September 3 hearing is a violation of Article 67 of the Criminal Code of Yugoslavia.

[67] Human Rights Watch/Helsinki interview in Peć, January 1994.

a group with an intention to use force or unconstitutional means to sever a part of Yugoslavia.[68]

At his trial on January 14, 1994, Mr. Čukaj insisted that he had signed the "confession" while in police custody out of fear for his life. He further testified that he had listed his two best friends as members of this group because he knew that they would understand why he had to name them.

No evidence was presented at the trial that confirmed the prosecutor's accusations. Mr. Čukaj's two friends were both abroad at that time and there were no other witnesses. The prosecutor's only "proof" of Mr. Čukaj's alleged criminal activities was his first statement given at the police station. The court sentenced Mr. Čukaj to four years in prison.

Sadri Shala and Ymer Shala

Sadri Shala, age sixty-two, and his son, Ymer Shala, age thirty, from the village of Dobra Voda, near Klina, owned the house in which the October 1, 1991 meeting took place.[69] Both men were arrested on September 9, 1993. Police badly beat both men during the first days of their detention.

Authorities accused the Shalas of aiding and abetting a criminal gathering for enemy activities by hosting the October 1, 1991 meeting. Their hearing before an investigative judge took place on September 14, six days after their arrest.

At their trial on January 14 and January 28, 1994, Judge Živojin Cvjeić refused to allow the Shalas to speak about the torture they had suffered while in custody. Sadri Shala identified a police officer in the courtroom as one of those who had beaten him, but the court ignored his remarks. The prison medical records for the two defendants, dated September 11, 1993, however, showed that both men had multiple

---

[68] *Indictment of F. Čukaj, S. Shala, Y. Shala and A. Lajci*, Peć, November 23, 1993. Fisnik Čujah was indicted under Article 136, paragraph 1 to Article 116 of the Yugoslav Criminal Code (grouping for enemy activities).

[69] Sadri and Ymer Shala were indicted under Article 136, paragraph 1 to Article 116, paragraph 1 and Article 24 of the Yugoslav Criminal Code (aiding others in grouping for enemy activities).

bruises. The court sentenced Sadri Shala to three years in prison, and Ymer Shala to two years.

Ali Lajci

Ali Lajci, age thirty-nine, from a village near Peć, is a former political prisoner. As one of the organizers of the 1981 anti-government demonstrations, he had been previously sentenced to fifteen years in prison. Lajci was arrested on September 7, 1993 at 4 A.M.. Police searched his house but found nothing. Lajci recalled:

> I spent three nights and three days handcuffed to a radiator at the police station without sleep, food or water. The policemen took turns beating and interrogating me about this meeting. They would make me lie on my stomach [while] three or four of them at a time would beat me over [my] entire body and feet. ... Then they took me before the investigative judge, but no one told me that he was a judge. I thought he was yet another policeman because this was in the police station.[70]

Lajci had been a guest at the October 1, 1991 meeting. His presence was enough for the prosecutor to indict him under Article 202, Paragraph 1 of the Criminal Code of Serbia.[71] Lajci was released in early December 1993, but the charges against him were not dropped. Later the court sentenced him to eight months in prison.

---

[70] Human Rights Watch/Helsinki interview in Peć, January 1994.

[71] Ali Lajci was indicted under Article 202, Para. 1 of the Criminal Code of Serbia:

> Who is aware of the preparations for a crime that, if committed, brings a punishment of five years and over, and does not report it to the authorities while it is still possible to prevent it from happening, and the crime is attempted or committed, shall be sentenced up to one year.

THE MILITARIZATION OF KOSOVO

YUGOSLAV ARMY MISTREATMENT OF CIVILIANS

Serbian officials contend that military and police guards in border areas only shoot at fleeing Albanians when justified — to apprehend a dangerous, armed suspect, and/or to prevent a border crossing. On the other hand, Albanians argue that the police and army at the border shoot first and ask questions later. They point to numerous examples in which the military shot without warning at people walking near the border. Although in many cases those involved were in fact trying to sneak across the border (as it is virtually impossible for Albanians to cross the border legally) they were not engaged in violence.[1]

As the U.S. State Department observed in its *Country Reports on Human Rights Practices for 1993* for Serbia and Montenegro:

> In a series of incidents along the Serbian-Albanian border, Serbian border guards were responsible for the deaths of fourteen Albanian citizens in Albania.[2] Serbian authorities defended their behavior, claiming that those killed were on the Serbian side of the border and had crossed it illegally, possibly for acts of terrorism. Smuggling is rife in the area, but the authorities appear to have used deadly force with little effort to apprehend the suspected border violators. In an effort to excuse the

---

[1] According to the regulations, citizens of Yugoslavia must obtain an exit visa from the Yugoslav police to visit Albania. However, it is almost impossible for Kosovo Albanians to obtain this visa. Those Kosovo Albanians who travel to Albania usually do so via a third-state in Western Europe. In addition, Serbian authorities have refused to issue passports to several hundred former political prisoners. They include Adem Demaqi, a prominent Albanian political leader, human rights activist and journalist who spent twenty-eight years in prison for his political beliefs.

[2] Only in January 1994, two more Albanian citizens were killed by the Serbian border guards.

killings following one incident, a senior Serbian official said that the Serbian border guards were inexperienced.[3]

Most of the army killings of Kosovo Albanians have occurred in this manner on the Albanian border. Human Rights Watch/Helsinki has been unable to confirm the number of people killed in such incidents — estimates range between eight and fourteen men killed in the past two years.[4] However, all sources agree that the number of incidents has increased in the past year, and killings in border areas have spread to the Macedonian border as well. One such incident is documented below.

On September 7, 1993 at about 12:30 P.M., two regular Yugoslav army soldiers shot two young Albanian men who were grazing their cows in the mountains near the unmarked border with Macedonia, an area where local peasants bring their animals to graze. Banush Sadiku, a nineteen-year-old Albanian, was killed and Fekir Fejza, also nineteen-years old, was critically wounded.

Two shepherds were eyewitnesses to the shooting. Twenty-five-year-old Bahri had been tending animals with his fifty-eight-year-old uncle, Milaim, when he heard machine gun fire:

> We lay down on the ground, because we thought they were shooting at us. ... When the shooting stopped, I saw Banush Sadiku sitting on the ground. I shouted to him "Go away!" and he just waved his hand at me. Then I saw the soldiers. There were two of them, in uniforms. The soldiers yelled at me and my uncle, "Go away, you two."

Milaim added:

> The two soldiers that were shooting were about 150 meters from us. When one of them said, "Go away from there," the other one

---

[3] U.S. Department of State, *Country Reports on Human Rights Practices for 1993* (February 1994).

[4] Human Rights Watch/Helsinki interviews with the Council on Human Rights of Kosova and the Kosova Helsinki Committee, in Priština, September-October 1993.

said "Go away from here." We didn't know what to do. ... When I saw Banush, I said to my nephew, "They're not shooting at us, they're shooting at other people." ... I didn't know whether Banush was wounded, he was just sitting. But when he tried to move, he fell down. He was about fifty to sixty meters from us — we were closer to the border than he was.

I wanted to go and try to help him and Bahri wanted to go with me. But when the soldiers saw that I was trying to go to him, they shouted, "Go away, or we will kill you too." The other soldier said to his friend, "No, leave him be, because he's good to kill." After that, I was afraid to go to Banush.

I saw the sheep up on the hill near the border and I went to get the sheep, but I didn't allow Bahri to go with me because I was afraid they would kill him. When I went to the sheep, I saw four or five other soldiers and they shouted at me, "Where are you going?" I said, "Can't you see? I'm going to get my sheep." They yelled insults at me.

While Milaim retrieved his sheep, his nephew Bahri hid from the soldiers in one of the shepherd's huts lining the hill. Milaim and Bahri remember that at this time, about a half-an-hour after the first burst of machine gun fire, they heard a solitary shot. Milaim then went to retrieve his cows which had scattered further down the hill:

I walked about 300 or 400 meters and I noticed someone crawling. When he saw me, he tried to escape from me, but I shouted to him, "Don't be afraid." When I came closer to him, I recognized him as Fekir. I asked him whether he was alone, or whether he was with someone, but he couldn't answer me because he was wounded in the mouth. I asked him at whom the soldiers had shot that solitary shot, and he tried to say that they had shot at him ... I took him by the shoulders and carried him to a hut. From time to time he lost consciousness.

At the hut, Milaim tried to give the wounded man first aid. About a half hour later, **Bahri** arrived at the hut, joined by two other young men. The men rolled Fekir onto an improvised stretcher and carried him to the nearby village of Firaja/Firajë. Bahri remembered:

> He was bleeding a lot. He was wounded in his neck and jaw. When we arrived at the village, we got a car and drove as fast as we could to the hospital. The police stopped us on the way and asked us what had happened. When they saw the wounded man, they said, "Where are you going with this man?" I said, "We are carrying him to the hospital." They didn't allow us to take him to Uroševac or Priština. They told us that we had to go to a clinic in Štrpce [a Serbian area and paramilitary stronghold] instead.

At the clinic, two policemen were waiting for the men. The police stood guard while Bahri and the other men carried Fekir into the emergency room. According to Bahri,

> In the emergency room, they didn't do anything for him. Three nurses, a doctor and two policemen were inside and they shouted to me, "Where did you find him?" One of those two policemen told me that I had to go with him to the police station. ... [At the police station], they started to interrogate me. They asked me, "Why were [Fekir and Banush] going up there [on the hill near the border]?" I answered that they were with cows. They said that they hadn't been with cows, that they were trying to get over the border.[5]

Eventually, the police allowed Bahri to return to his village.

Meanwhile, villagers in Firaja and Brod who had learned that soldiers had shot and killed Banush attempted to retrieve his body. But, according to the villagers, a large group of soldiers stopped them about 1,000 meters from the spot where they could see the body lying. The

---

[5] The army later told family members that they had shot at the boys because they had attempted to cross the border illegally.

villagers waited for about seven hours in the hills for permission to go further, but the soldiers continued to turn them away. As night fell, the villagers eventually left and went home. The next day, the soldiers told some of the shepherds living in huts in the mountain that they could go retrieve the body. At 5:00 P.M. on September 8th — over twenty-six hours after villagers first attempted to retrieve the body, a long procession of villagers carried the body down the mountain.

The villagers believe that soldiers had moved Banush's body from the place where he was shot to a location approximately fifty meters closer to the border. Indeed, Milaim, the old man who had witnessed the shooting, testified that he was among the group that had finally retrieved the body and that, "strangely enough, Banush was no longer lying in the spot where he had been shot." In support of this thesis, doctors who examined the body noted rope burns on the dead man's neck and scratches across his torso, indicating that he had been dragged by a rope around his neck.[6]

Fekir survived the shooting. According to his brother, Beqir, Fekir was eventually brought to a hospital in Priština:

> When I learned that my brother had been shot [on September 8th, a day after the incident], I immediately went to Priština to see him. ... There was an Albanian doctor who was treating him. ... They had given him stitches and nothing else, because they didn't have the medical supplies. We had to bring all of the drugs for him to the hospital. After about five days, they operated on him and two weeks later he was released. ... Now, he's staying at my home. He can't eat for himself so we have to feed him. Almost every night, he wakes up screaming. He is very afraid.

On the 12th of October, soldiers returned to the same area and told the shepherds they found there that they would no longer be

---

[6] The testimony of the doctors and other villagers who saw the body was supported by photographs and video tapes which illustrated such rope burns and scratches. Human Rights Watch/Helsinki interviews and inspection of photographs and videotapes in Uroševac in September 1993.

permitted to take their animals up into the mountains to graze, nor would they be able to live in the huts dotting the mountain.[7]

UPDATE ON REGULAR MILITARY AND PARAMILITARY FORCES AND ARMED SERBIAN CIVILIANS

With heavily armed army and police troops patrolling the streets, Kosovo has the air of an occupied area. While the Council on Human Rights in Kosovo estimates that there are now 40,000 to 60,000 Yugoslav troops in Kosovo, and 40,000 police officers, official Serbian statistics claim that these estimates are at best ten times too high.[8] Regardless of the exact figures, the extremely visible police and army presence dominates marketplaces and village streets, a constant reminder of who controls life in Kosovo. Belgrade authorities have maintained that the increased stationing of armed forces in Kosovo is "necessary in order to eliminate all risks and dangers that result from the complicated and unfavorable ethnic composition" in Kosovo.[9]

Since 1990, police and military forces in Kosovo have been nearly 100 percent Serbian. From March to September 1990, 3,400 Albanian police officers were dismissed from work.[10] Others resigned in protest to the suspension of the Kosovo government and parliament and other "emergency measures." In July 1991, the Serbian parliament passed a law that gave itself the authority to bring in policemen from all over

---

[7] The peasants had previously lived in the huts in the mountains for months at a time during the warmer months.

[8] Official Serbian statistics set the number of troops much lower, at 4,000 regular personnel and conscripts and 1,200 military reservists. *Report of the CSCE Conflict Prevention Center Fact-Finding Mission to Kosovo*, Vienna, June 5, 1992, p. 4.

[9] "CSCE Delegation Reports on Political Tension," Vienna Kurier report of June 12, 1992, as reported in FBIS on June 12, 1992.

[10] Human Rights Watch/Helsinki interview with Januz Tërstena, Independent Trade Union of Police of Kosova in Belgrade, January 1994.

Yugoslavia to replace the dismissed Albanians.[11] Today, most of the officers are Serbs and Montenegrins from Serbia proper or Montenegro. Others are professional police officers who were brought in from Croatia and Bosnia-Hercegovina.

In addition to the regular police and army, paramilitary forces and armed Serb civilians regularly patrol villages and cities in Kosovo, harassing and intimidating non-Serbs. The presence of "irregular" troops is so strong in border areas that many villagers who spoke with Human Rights Watch/Helsinki there spoke of "the military" without differentiating between regular army troops and paramilitary forces. "There are all types of uniforms," a shepherd said, "And all we know is they are all after us."[12]

One of the most notorious of the accused war criminals in the wars in Croatia and Bosnia-Hercegovina, Željko Ražnatović, also known as Arkan, has made Kosovo his stronghold. According to Albanians in Uroševac, Arkan and his paramilitary troop — the Tigers — have chosen their town and the nearby village of Štrpce/Shtërpcë as one of their bases. Moreover, Vojislav Šešelj, the president of the Serbian Radical Party (Srpska Radikalna Stranka — SRS) and leader of a paramilitary formation, is currently a member of the Yugoslav Parliament. As the owner of a Serbian football club in Priština, Arkan is spotted frequently around the Grand Hotel Priština, which his supporters have taken over for a headquarters. Arkan is a member of the Serbian Parliament and the head of the Party of Serbian Unity.

Up until mid-1993, Šešelj's paramilitary troop — the Serbian Četniks, also known as the "White Eagles" and by other names — had a strong and visible presence in Kosovo as well. After his apparent split with the Serbian president Slobodan Milosević, Šešelj made few public appearances. However, according to the villagers in northern Kosovo, Šešelj's troops, identifiable by the insignia they wear on their uniforms, took part in the raids on their towns in the summer of 1993.

Also during the summer of 1993, Albanians sighted Šešelj and/or his supporters parading down the streets of Priština, Prizren and Mitrovica among other towns. An Albanian political activist in Prizren,

[11] *Official Gazette of Serbia* 44/91, July 25, 1991.

[12] Human Rights Watch/Helsinki interview in Uroševac, September 1993. Name withheld to protect witness.

for example, reported seeing both Arkan's and Šešelj's supporters in Prizren:

> Two months ago [in July 1993] Arkan came to Prizren with his boys. He made a clear statement that he was here. Šešelj was in Prizren too [this summer]. He held a rally at which he said that he would kick out all of the Albanians. Šešelj's supporters were there; they weren't in uniforms, but we all know that they are armed.[13]

Albanian human rights groups allege that the northwestern city of Peć serves as one base for paramilitary groups. According to the LDK of Peć and members of the Human Rights Council of Pejë, three kinds of army barracks exist in their city: one for regular police, one for the regular army, and one for paramilitary troops. Several Albanians interviewed independently corroborated this account. As one clerk in Peć said:

> There are so many Serbs with guns around here, in uniform, not in uniform, paramilitary, not paramilitary. It is impossible to tell who is who. Many of these men are dressed in civilian clothes. They don't publicly show any weapons. They just hang around the army barracks. Some of them might even live there. We're not sure the extent of their activities — it is too risky to confirm.[14]

Paramilitary groups reportedly conduct their training exercises and parade openly, free from any interference by the regular police or army. Pasjane/Pasjan, an area near Gnjilane, reportedly serves as one paramilitary training ground. A local Albanian leader told Human Rights Watch/Helsinki that "they practice there every day. It is common knowledge here. We know that they are paramilitary by their uniforms

---

[13] Human Rights Watch/Helsinki interview in Prizren, October 1993. Name with held to protect witness.

[14] Human Rights Watch/Helsinki interview in Peć, October 1993. Name withheld to protect witness.

and the emblem they wear."[15]   On Albanian holidays, paramilitary
troops have been sighted parading down the streets of Gnjilane and other
Albanian towns and villages.

In addition to harassment by paramilitary troops, several
Albanians have reported abuses by armed civilians.   While in many
instances Human Rights Watch/Helsinki has been unable to determine
the exact source of Serbian civilians' arms, some reports point to the
Yugoslav army and police as main suppliers.[16]   Human Rights
Watch/Helsinki has reasons to believe that when the (former) Yugoslavia's
authorities disbanded the territorial defense units[17] in late 1980s, their
outdated weapons were handed over to the police and the Serbian
civilians in many areas, including Kosovo. Witnesses claim that in 1987
and 1988, army and police distributed weapons off the backs of trucks to
Kosovo Serbs, without permits for possession of arms.   In many cases,

---

[15] Human Rights Watch/Helsinki interview in Gnjilane, October 1993. Name
withheld to protect witness.

[16] See, e.g., The International Helsinki Federation, *From Autonomy to
Colonization: Human Rights in Kosovo 1989-1993*, November 1993.

[17] After World War II and during Tito's reign, the official Yugoslav position
maintained that Yugoslavia, as a non-aligned state, was surrounded by external
enemies, such as the North Atlantic Treaty Organization (NATO) to the west and
the Warsaw Pact to the east. In light of these "threats," Yugoslavia had to be
prepared to defend its "territorial integrity, unity and independence."   In
preparation for possible attacks from "outside enemies," weapons for the general
population were stored at the local level throughout the country. The weapons
were purchased from workers' revenues at local enterprises and kept in various
storage areas throughout each locality. Each of Yugoslavia's six constituent
republics maintained a territorial defense structure, which included a civilian
security force (civilna zaštisa) and a local reserve militia. All former soldiers who
served in the federal army could be called up to serve as reserve police officers
for the republican force or members of the local territorial defense (teritorijalna
obrana-TO) unit. The TO's weapon's could be distributed by the republican
government, in consultation with the federal army and the federal government.

one man told Human Rights Watch/Helsinki, it was not possible to reject a gun. "They knocked on your door and left a gun," he said.[18]

As Human Rights Watch/Helsinki reported previously, the Serbian government has been aware of the distribution of weapons to civilians in Kosovo since at least May 1991, when the matter was discussed in the Yugoslav parliament.[19] In any event, from the many incidents of abuse by armed Serbian civilians, it is clear that they are indeed well armed and that Serbian authorities have done little to discourage their harassment of Albanians. For example, Human Rights Watch/Helsinki spoke with several families in northern Kosovo who testified that armed Serbian civilians had shot at them in attempts to chase them off their land.

Human Rights Watch/Helsinki has received several reports of police and regular army troops working in conjunction with paramilitary groups and armed civilians. In raiding one house in northern Kosovo, for instance, police said "We're not just police. We're Šešelj's police."[20] In another case reported in greater detail above, a police officer who was attempting to throw an Albanian family out of its house appeared at the door on several occasions with comrades wearing different uniforms. Such reports of regular police working alongside paramilitary groups, if accurate, present a particularly disturbing development.

---

[18] Human Rights Watch/Helsinki interviews in Kosovo, November 1993.

[19] See Helsinki Watch, *Yugoslavia: Human Rights Abuses in Kosovo 1990-1992*, October 1992, p. 52.

[20] Human Rights Watch/Helsinki interview in Mitrovica, September 1993. Name withheld to protect witness.

RESTRICTIONS ON FREEDOM OF THE PRESS AND PROSECUTION OF JOURNALISTS[1]

By law, the press is free in Yugoslavia and individuals are free to criticize the government. In reality, however, the state maintains tight control over the media, both indirectly, through intimidation and harassment of journalists critical of the regime, and directly by restricting access to broadcast frequencies and through a massive purge of dissident journalists. Although the situation is bad in all of Serbia,[2] conditions are even worse in Kosovo.

BROADCASTING

The situation with Albanian-language broadcasting has been dismal since July 5, 1990, when police occupied the Radio-Television

---

[1] The following is a short summary and update of the situation facing journalists in Kosovo. For a more complete history and details of abuses prior to 1993, see Helsinki Watch, *Yugoslavia: Human Rights Abuses in Kosovo 1990-1992*, October 1992, p. 29-37; see also Helsinki Watch, *Threats to Press Freedoms: A Report Prepared for the Free Media Seminar (Commission on Security and Cooperation in Europe)*, Vol. 5, Issue 21, November 1993. The information in this section is gathered from continual Human Rights Watch/Helsinki monitoring of the media in Kosovo.

[2] Last January alone, Radio/TV Serbia forced out more than 1,000 workers on forced vacations ostensibly because of economic difficulties, but actually due to their political beliefs. This fall, the Supreme Court in Belgrade reversed a decision of a lower court holding the forced layoffs to be illegal, thus permitting Radio-TV Serbia to lay off dissenting journalists at will. State-controlled radio and television provide the sole source of news for most citizens. Although anti-establishment radio and television stations exist, they are concentrated mainly in Belgrade and other large urban areas in Serbia proper. Accordingly, most of the population still depends on Radio-TV Serbia, a mouthpiece for Milošević that promotes ethnic hatred. See Helsinki Watch, *Threats to Press Freedoms: A Report Prepared for the Free Media Seminar (Commission on Security and Cooperation in Europe)*, Vol. 5, Issue 21, November 1993.

building in Priština and prevented employees from entering the premises.[3] Serbia imposed "special measures" on Radio-Television Priština, replacing the editor-in-chief with a Serb handpicked from Belgrade.[4] Subsequently, about 1,300 employees were fired for alleged disloyalty to the state.[5] Since then, no independent Albanian radio and television stations have existed in Kosovo.

Today, the only regular Albanian-language television programs in all of Kosovo are news bulletins, broadcast twice daily, translated directly from Serbian programming. Similarly, the only regular Albanian-language radio news broadcasts consist of translations from *Tanjug*, the official Yugoslav news agency.[6] The Secretary of Information for Kosovo, Boško Drobnjak, points to such programming as an illustration of Serbs' commitment to Albanian speakers:

> We recognize the right to be informed in one's own language, in line with international laws and domestic laws. We've gone even a step further, allowing for not only a possibility of minorities being informed in their own language, but also the state is obliged to give financial assistance for minority-language programming.

---

[3] Prior to 1990, Radio-Television Priština provided work for 1,800 people, mainly Albanians.

[4] According to the Minister of Information:
> The special measures were put into place due to extreme requests by Albanian TV/Radio. They didn't want to accept state measures. The editor-in-chief was removed and a new one was brought in who was willing to obey the policies of the owner [the state]. The problem with the previous editor-in-chief was that he said that Albanians shouldn't recognize Serbia, that they should boycott all laws from Serbia.

Human Rights Watch/Helsinki interview in Priština, in September 1993.

[5] Serbian authorities laid off additional Albanian journalists under a new Law on Public Information, enacted in March 1991, see *Official Gazette of Serbia* 19/91, March 29, 1991.

[6] After the takeover of Radio-Television Priština, Serbian authorities shut down six other Albanian-language local radio stations.

> The media founded by the state can apply for and
> receive such help. For example, Albanian-language
> programming on Radio/TV Priština, a state station, is
> [paid for by the state].

Albanians, however, dismiss the programming on Radio/TV Priština as
Serbian propaganda. Most Albanians instead obtain their information
from radio and television Tirana, as well as the BBC, Voice of America
and Deutsche Welle Albanian-language programs. Radio and television
broadcasts from Albania are frequently jammed in order to prevent
Kosovo Albanians from receiving them.

Mr. Drobnjak insists that there are no state-imposed roadblocks
preventing the establishment of new Albanian-language television and
radio stations:

> The media is free. To the extent that there are any
> requirements, they are reasonable. You have to make a
> request to the minister of information, state the nature
> of the media, the owner, the editor-in-chief, the kind of
> program.

The Secretary of Information says that he has had no requests for the
creation of new television and radio stations in Kosovo. Albanian leaders
cite economic difficulties as the main barrier to attempting to establish a
new station.

THE PRESS AND PUBLISHING

The printed press in Kosovo faced a similar decline beginning in
1990. At that time, there were some forty Albanian-language newspapers
and periodicals.[7] The Rilindja (Renaissance) publishing house published
three main newspapers — *Rilindja* in Albanian (the only Albanian-
language daily), *Jedinstvo* in Serbian and *Tan* in Turkish. In August 1990,
Serbian authorities banned the newspaper *Rilindja*, laying off journalists
and other support staff who refused to sign a pledge of loyalty to the new
management.

---

[7] Information drawn from the Kosovo Helsinki Committee.

In response, the editors of *Bujku* (Farmer), an Albanian-language agricultural newspaper published by the Rilindja publishing house, gradually transformed the publication into a general daily newspaper with a circulation between 25-30,000. Since then, however, *Bujku* has been beset by a host of economic difficulties which limit its size and scope. The operators of *Bujku* believe that these difficulties have only been exacerbated by the newspaper's tenuous relationship with Panorama, the Serbian publishing company that controls printing costs for all newspapers in Kosovo.

The Serbian assembly created "Panorama" in November 1992 to succeed the Rilindja publishing house. When the law was enforced in May 1993, Panorama immediately assumed control of Rilindja's physical assets[8] and authority over the latter's printing, distribution and banking operations. Operating the only newspaper printing facilities in Kosovo, Panorama now acts as the umbrella company for all papers in Kosovo.

The overall effect of the new Panorama management is tighter state control over the Albanian-language press, as the Serbian government directs all editorial and employment policies. In May 1993, Panorama ordered the closing of the only regular, Albanian-language political weekly, *Zëri* (Voice).[9] In protest of the creation of Panorama and the abolition of *Zëri*, Adem Demaqi, then the editor-in-chief of *Zëri* and a prominent political activist,[10] joined by almost 250 Albanian journalists and sympathizers, held a hunger strike in June 1993. They called the strike off after the CSCE mission in Kosovo intervened to mediate the situation. Nevertheless, Panorama has still refused to relinquish control of Rilindja's property and assets.

Bujku now publishes 10,000 copies six times a week as part of the Panorama publishing company, on which it depends for printing and distribution. The price of *Bujku* is higher than other daily newspapers in

---

[8] The value of Rilindja's property (an eighteen-story building, equipment, printing facilities, 470 kiosks, etc.) is estimated at 2.3 million U.S. dollars.

[9] *Zëri*, once published by the Socialist Youth of Yugoslavia, became an influential — and for a long time the only — political weekly in the region. Its offices are located in the Panorama building and its status is almost identical to that of *Bujku*. It manages to maintain its circulation at about 30,000 copies.

[10] Adem Demaqi had spent almost twenty-eight years in prison.

Serbia.[11] As operation costs escalate in relation to sales, *Bujku* loses
money daily and its continued publication remains precarious. Rusdi
Demiri, editor-in-chief of *Bujku* explained:

> We pay Panorama $2000 for rent of our own offices in
> the Rilindja building, printing expenses and distribution
> costs. By the time they return the money from the sales,
> we loose $200 to $500 per edition.[12]

For the time being, *Bujku* survives largely on private donations.

Over the past two years, several other Albanians papers have
disappeared due to financial problems, and many attempts to start new
publications have failed. According to Boško Drobnjak (the Kosovo
Secretary for Information), "in the last two or three years, there have
been about 17 independent newspapers; some are published for about a
year, usually less, and then they all go out of business." Recently however,
with considerable support from the Soros Foundation, several new and
resurrected Albanian journals have begun publication, from a social
science journal to a handful of children's publications.

The most significant of these are *Forumi* (Forum), a political
weekly under the editorship of Adem Demaqi, and Veton Surroi's *Koha*
(Time). *Forumi* is an independent paper, with no affiliation with any
existing political party. As of now, it writes about Albanian and Serbian
issues and is aimed at a local readership. The staff plans to expand and
sell the newspaper abroad. Dissident journalist Veton Surroi resurrected
Koha in February 1994; the paper had previously existed for nine months,
September 1990-June 1991. According to Mr. Surroi, *Koha* is a weekly
news magazine designed for a middle-class readership and Albanian-

---

[11] The Minister of Information, however, argues that Panorama has nothing
to do with the price of *Bujku*. Indeed, technically *Bujku* sets its own price;
however, that price is influenced by the cost of printing which, in turn, is set by
Panorama.

[12] Human Rights Watch/Helsinki interview in Priština, November 1993.

speaking intellectuals which seeks to create a "polycentric" magazine covering Balkan, European and world issues.[13]

Turkish-language papers have suffered problems similar to those encountered by the Albanian-language press. The sole newspaper published regularly, *Tan*, carries only news and comments translated from Serbian. According to Sezair Shaipi, the head of the Turkish Peoples' Party in Kosovo, "over the past year or two there has not been a single report in *Tan* about the problems of the Kosovo Turks. We have tried to set up a weekly or biweekly magazine, but we still cannot afford it."[14]

No foreign journals are available for sale in Kosovo. According to Mr. Drobnjak, Serbian law does not prohibit or even regulate the sale of foreign newspapers and magazines in Kosovo, including those from Albania. He blamed the U.N.-imposed sanctions for the lack of foreign newspapers. In contrast, Albanians report that they would be afraid to sell foreign papers, especially those printed in the Albanian language. And several Albanian human rights activists and political activists reported incidents at the Kosovo border in which police detained them and confiscated whatever foreign publications they were carrying.

With Serbian control over printing and publishing, very few books have been published in the Albanian language in Kosovo in the past three years. Albanians have opened small, private publishing companies to combat official policies. The law allows private presses to publish books and specialized magazines, but not newspapers. Nevertheless, the Serbian police raided one such company and confiscated the entire run of Rexhep Ismail's book *Kosovo and the Albanians in Former Yugoslavia*. Albanians working abroad and at home also have tried to publish some Albanian literature and school books through private presses. However, these efforts have also met with financial difficulties.

UPDATE ON PURGES AND HARASSMENT OF JOURNALISTS

At the end of 1993, most Albanian journalists were either unemployed or engaged as stringers for the foreign press or *Bujku*. Most of those who were working were doing so "illegally" in the view of

---

[13] Human Rights Watch/Helsinki interview with Veton Surroi in Priština, November 1993.

[14] Human Rights Watch/Helsinki interview in Prizren, December 1993.

Serbian authorities, since they refuse to be accredited by the Yugoslav Ministry of Information in Belgrade, as required by law.

Human Rights Watch/Helsinki spoke with many journalists throughout Kosovo who had recently been harassed and interrogated by the police. In Peć, for example, police reportedly threatened to kill one journalist if he didn't stop writing. In several areas, journalists report being brought into the police station for "informative discussions." To the extent that authorities ever press charges against journalists, they are usually for "spreading false information,"[15] "endangering the territorial integrity of Yugoslavia,"[16] or "inciting national hatred."[17]

People who read Albanian publications are also harassed. According to the LDK of Peć, for example, police forced a man to eat the front page of the paper which boasted a photograph of Rugova.[18] And, in addition, foreign journalists have reported incidents of harassment and intimidation. For example, in November 1993 police in Prizren harassed and detained a British journalist and a Human Rights Watch/Helsinki researcher who had been attending a political trial.

---

[15] Article 218 of the Criminal Code of Serbia.

[16] Article 116 of the Criminal Code of Yugoslavia.

[17] Article 134 of the Criminal Code of Yugoslavia.

[18] Human Rights Watch/Helsinki interview in Peć, October 1993.

EMPLOYMENT DISCRIMINATION

UPDATE ON EMERGENCY LAWS AND MASS LAYOFFS

Beginning in 1990, the Serbian Parliament adopted a series of laws which permitted discrimination against Albanians in employment (and in other aspects of daily life) on several grounds. The Program for the Establishment of Peace, Liberty, Equality, Democracy and Prosperity in the Autonomous Province of Kosovo[1] provided for the immediate replacement of Albanians who were dismissed for striking. The law also endorsed the principle that Serbia should pass further laws encouraging the recruitment of Serbian and Montenegrin workers in Kosovo.

On July 26, 1990, Serbian authorities passed a Law on Labor Relations in Special Circumstances[2] which made official the policy of recruiting of non-Albanians and gave the directors of enterprises the right to impose disciplinary measures upon their workers.[3] This law became the cornerstone of a Serbian policy of mass dismissal of Albanian workers on grounds of ethnicity and/or political activities. For example, Serbian employers pointed to this law in appointing "temporary management teams" that in turn required workers to sign loyalty oaths, stating their

---

[1] *Official Gazette of Serbia*, 15/90, March 30, 1990. Among many provisions not detailed here, the Program also declared that Serbian was the only official language throughout the Republic. (Many Albanian teachers, doctors and others were subsequently fired for refusing to abide by this rule). It also announced that in the following school year, several thousand Serb and Montenegrin students would be enrolled in Priština University (thus reducing the number of Albanian students). In addition, the Program called for a uniform education system throughout Serbia (see following section of this report), the reduction of the Kosovo (Albanian) birth rate, the strengthening and equipping of the police force (ethnically pure police units were formed), etc.

[2] *Official Gazette of Serbia*, No. 40/90, July 26, 1990. This Law, in effect, also outlawed strikes by giving managers the right to fire workers who "are late or absent from work for two days of the week," as well as those who are disruptive at work or leave work voluntarily.

[3] See *Situation of Human Rights in the Former Yugoslavia*, Tadeusz Mazowiecki, Special Rapporteur of the UN Commission on Human Rights, February 10, 1993.

acceptance of Serbian control. Numerous workers were dismissed after they refused to sign such oaths.

As a part of the same process, over 500 families have been evicted from their homes.[4] By law, former employees could demand apartments back from the workers, since they had left their jobs "voluntarily." Thus, the police repeatedly evicted those who refused to leave their homes.

In March 1993, the Serbian Assembly officially abolished the Law on Labor Relations in Special Circumstances. This move, however, had little practical impact. The Assembly did not overthrow previous decisions based on the old law, nor did it reinstate the estimated 112,000 to 115,000 Albanians who had lost their jobs.[5] Workers from Montenegro and Serbia still enjoy special treatment by law, regulation and practice. Moreover, while some Serb authorities in Kosovo have admitted to Human Rights Watch/Helsinki that the loyalty oaths were a mistake and have stated that employees who previously refused to sign such oaths will be hired back, few Albanians want to reapply for their old positions in unfriendly environments.

Some of the industries crippled by the layoffs include the mining industry — over 12,000 Albanian workers were laid off from the Trepča Mines (in Mitrovica) alone [6] — the construction industry (10,000 fired), iron and steel industry (13,000 fired), and the textile industry (13,000 fired), with some plants entirely closed and operations moved to Serbia. Other workers hit hard by the layoffs include Albanians working for the Serbian government in any capacity, including clerks at state run enterprises and government offices, doctors in state hospitals, school

---

[4] See Helsinki Watch, *Yugoslavia: Human Rights Abuses in Kosovo 1990-1992*, October 1992, pp. 48-49. Most apartments in the urban areas of former Yugoslavia belonged to the state, municipalities or state-owned enterprises. After an employee worked for a company for a certain number of years, an apartment would be allocated to him. The company (or the state) remained the legal owner, while the worker had "the right to occupy" an apartment. Rump Yugoslavia's law allows workers to buy the apartments they occupied, usually under favorable conditions. That right is, as a rule, denied Albanians in Serbia.

[5] These statistics were provided by the Kosovo Helsinki Committee.

[6] For testimony of the miners, see Helsinki Watch, *Yugoslavia: Human Rights Abuses in Kosovo 1990-1992*, October 1992, pp. 38-39.

teachers and university professors, telephone operators, journalists at state-operated media, and heavy laborers in state-run industries.

The layoffs have leveled off recently — perhaps because there are so few people left to be fired.[7] Only an estimated twenty percent of the adult Albanian population is still employed; nearly all of them work in the private sector.[8]

The example of Elez Nikci, a ballet dancer from Priština, best illustrates how thorough the government purges of Albanian employees are. Mr. Nikci explained:

> The Priština theater consisted of three departments: ballet, Serbian [language] drama, and Albanian [language] drama. Twenty-three Albanians and five Macedonians worked in the ballet department. We often had guest dancers from other countries. In January 1991, the authorities dismissed the theater management and appointed Mirko Zarić as our director.

> At that time, we were preparing a performance. When the new director saw it, he said that there was too much folklore and that we should start working on "Banović Strahinja," a typical Serbian performance. We responded that we would start working on that after we performed the ballet that we had already prepared. Zarić said in a television interview that ballet is "a state symbol," and that there cannot be "two ballets in one country."[9]

In November 1991, the Priština theater's temporary management team dismissed the ballet section. The Albanian dancers were subsequently laid off and declared "technological excess." Mr. Nikci was finally dismissed on November 1, 1993, after twenty-two years of work.

---

[7] According to LDK leaders, as of September 1993, seventy percent of Albanian workers have been dismissed from work.

[8] Human Rights Watch/Helsinki interview with the Council on Human Rights in Priština, September 1993.

[9] Human Rights Watch/Helsinki interview in Priština, November 1993.

ECONOMIC IMPACT OF DISMISSALS

The mass dismissals have caused enormous hardship. As Serbian law does not grant welfare benefits to anyone dismissed from their jobs. An estimated 500,000 people remain without social or health insurance.[10] Many Albanian families now subsist entirely on solidarity funds gathered privately from Albanian organizations or, if they are lucky, from contributions sent from relatives living abroad.[11]

Still, according to the Alliance of Independent Trade Unions of Kosovo, over 60,000 families are living below the accepted poverty line. As many as 80,000 physically and mentally handicapped people depend entirely on solidarity funds (Albanian welfare funds), since they receive no aid from the state. As a result of the malnutrition which affects a large percent of the population, physicians have noted an increase in the number of cases of tuberculosis and hepatitis. Further, the dismissed Albanians have no health insurance and many cannot afford hospital treatment.[12]

In recent years, over 300,000 Albanians have left Kosovo, mostly for Germany, Switzerland and Scandinavian countries.[13] In January 1994, the Society for the Return of Albanians Working Abroad set this figure as high as 500,000.[14] As one Albanian demographer explained, "The first wave was mostly young men who wanted to avoid the draft.

---

[10] Human Rights Watch/Helsinki interview with Alliance of Independent Trade Unions in Priština, January 1994.

[11] See Helsinki Watch, *Yugoslavia: Human Rights Abuses in Kosovo 1990-1992*, October 1992, p. 47.

[12] Human Rights Watch/Helsinki interview with the Alliance of Independent Unions in Priština, January 1994.

[13] See *Human Rights Questions: Human Rights Situations and Reports of the Special Rapporteur and Representatives: The Situation of Human Rights in the Territory of the Former Yugoslavia.* Note by the Secretary General, United Nations General Assembly — Security Council, November 17, 1992.

[14] Human Rights Watch/Helsinki interview in Priština, January 1994.

The latest wave has been people trying to make a little money to send home to their families."[15]

Albanians have set up their own extensive welfare system to fight poverty.   One of the largest funds is administered through an organization called the Charity and Humanitarian Society of Mother Teresa (founded in 1990).[16] Mother Teresa chapters throughout Kosovo submit monthly requests to the main chapter for the amount of food, clothes and medicines needed. According to Jak Mita, a representative of Mother Teresa, the group distributes between 400 and 600 tons of food every month.[17]   Mr. Mita estimates that nearly 46,000 families (about 300,000 people) receive aid from Mother Teresa.

Mr. Mita reports difficulty in bringing food into Kosovo from the various humanitarian organizations throughout Europe that make regular donations. According to Mr. Mita, Serbian officials are to blame for the delay. Since official market inspectors must be present when trucks are unloaded to examine the produce, he says, this process often leads to long delays, causing food spoilage. Also, he contends, Serbian authorities attempt to skim what they can off of the humanitarian donations. "They asked us for ten percent of the food as a sample," Mr. Mita said, adding that "recently they wanted 2,000 kilograms of cheese for what they claimed to be 'biological tests.'"

---

[15] Human Rights Watch/Helsinki interview in Priština, October 1993.

[16] The LDK also directly administers a solidarity fund for Albanian teachers, doctors, and writers.

[17] Human Rights Watch/Helsinki interview in Priština, October 1993.

DISCRIMINATION IN EDUCATION

UPDATE ON MASS LAYOFFS OF ALBANIAN TEACHERS

In August of 1990, the Serbian parliament passed a series of laws that abolished the independence of the Kosovo educational system and instituted a new curriculum to be administered centrally from Belgrade.[1] Among other changes, the new curriculum expanded in the instruction in Serbian history and culture while simultaneously reducing instruction in the Albanian language and culture. In addition, new regulations were adopted that prohibited Albanian schoolchildren from entering a secondary school unless they passed examinations in Serbian language and literature.[2]

Many Albanian teachers refused to recognize the new curriculum and, as a result, Serbian authorities began demanding that teachers sign a loyalty oath. When most of the teachers refused to sign, they were dismissed. One of teachers at an Albanian Economic School explained:

---

[1] See *Situation of Human Rights in the Former Yugoslavia*, Tadeusz Mazowiecki, Special Rapporteur of the UN Commission on Human Rights, February 10, 1993, p. 35; *Official Gazette of Serbia* 45/90, August 7, 1990. See also *Official Gazette of Serbia*, 75/91, December 17, 1991. In the words of the Regional Secretary for Education Marinko Božović:

> According to the laws of the Republic of Serbia and of Yugoslavia, Albanians, Turks, and Muslims have the right to education in their own language, their own books, own professors, school programs, etc. Up until 1990, we did all of this. As of 1990, when Serbia became a unified country and the autonomy of Kosovo was abolished, the education council of Kosovo and Vojvodina were merged with the education council of Serbia. Now, instead of having three councils, we have one educational council.

Human Rights Watch/Helsinki interview in Priština, September 1993.

[2] According to official Serbian statistics, in 1988/89, there were 841 Albanian-language primary schools in Kosovo, with 13,257 Albanian teachers providing instruction for 303,035 pupils. The same year, sixty-six secondary schools and 3,485 teachers provided Albanian-language instruction for 63,842 pupils. *Statistical Yearbook of the Republic of Serbia*, Statistical Office, Belgrade, 1990.

They had termination notices prepared for each of us. They told us that we had to sign a paper saying that "I recognize the State of Serbia." Only one guy signed. In January 1991, they stopped paying us. But that January they gave us a lump payment of 3,000 [German] marks each. They tried to bribe us to come back with promises of increased pay. The teachers that remained got excellent money.[3]

The Kosovo Secretary of Education, Marinko Božović, however, flatly denies this account. According to him, schools never required a loyalty oath for teachers, but teachers were merely told to follow the prescribed program. He stated:

Not a single teacher has been fired. Not a single professor has been fired. In 1990, when the Albanians began boycotting the schools, they switched to their own [educational] system. Although I wanted to talk to them [to work things out], no one would talk.[4]

When pushed, he admitted that some teachers were fired, but claimed that these were exceptional cases:

Some teachers were fired for violating basic standards of human rights, the ones who took part in demonstrations advocating the overthrow of the government. These are the exceptions.[5]

Whatever the reason, the authorities began closing high schools, one by one, and then, in January 1991, stopped paying most Albanian high school teachers. In April 1991, the authorities stopped paying Albanian elementary school teachers. As of August 1991, all Albanian

---

[3] Human Rights Watch/Helsinki interview in Priština, September 1993.

[4] Human Rights Watch/Helsinki interview in Priština, September 1993.

[5] The Minister said that in 1993 he posted an advertisement for job offerings for Albanian teachers but no one responded.

high school teachers had been fired; as of October 1991, all Albanian teachers had been fired; only fifteen Albanian professors remained, and they all now teach in Serbian.

Throughout the 1991/92 school year, both Albanian primary and secondary schools remained closed and, in some cases, armed police guarded the empty buildings to ensure that they would not be put to use. However, in the 1992/93 school year, many primary schools re-opened, but the teachers were not paid by the state. With the beginning of the 1993/94 school year, the situation remained the same, with primary schools operating with unpaid teachers and nearly all secondary schools closed. In September 1993, 63,000 students tried to enter the secondary schools in Kosovo but they were blocked by police.

Albanian teachers have created an Association of Albanian Teachers to run a so-called "parallel system" of Albanian-language schools. According to the head of this organization, Rexhep Osmani, in the 1993/94 school year, 300,000 elementary school students are attending classes in school buildings with teachers not paid by the state.[6] Albanian children, however, attend lectures in the evening shifts after Serb children finish their classes. The Serbian dean of the Miloš Crnjanski elementary school in Priština was particularly inventive: he built brick walls along school halls to prevent any contact between children of different nationalities.

In the 1993/94 school year, since there is not enough room for all Albanian students in primary schools, 1,200 Albanian primary students attend classes in private homes.[7] In addition, because they are shut out of their schools altogether, 60,000 high school students attend classes in private homes.

According to Mr. Božović, Albanians pulled out of the state education system voluntarily:

> There are still laws that allow Albanians to be taught in
> their own language. However, as of 1990 and 1991,

---

[6] Mr. Božović pointed out that they use heat and electricity for free.

[7] Mr. Božović recognizes that many high school students attend class in private homes but contends that "there are no elementary schools in private homes." Human Rights Watch/Helsinki representatives, however, visited a private elementary school.

> Albanians have left the system and have established a
> parallel system independent of the state. They have their
> own teachers and their own management. They even
> issue documents saying "Republic of Kosova." ... The
> Albanians alone write their own programs now and we
> have no control over them.[8]

This "voluntary" parallel system, Mr. Božović asserted, was in clear
violation of the law.

Today, a total of 22,000 Albanian teachers do not receive any
income from the state. Albanians have organized a system of "self-
financing" to pay for their teachers. All Albanians who are employed, in
Kosovo or abroad, are requested to make voluntary contributions. The
suggested "voluntary tax" rate for this and other services run by the
Albanian "parallel government" is three percent of income. According to
one man in charge of the fund:

> We're trying to give teachers forty [German] marks a
> month, and professors at the university eighty-two to one
> hundred marks a month. This of course is not enough
> to survive ... right now it is all we can afford to give.
> Right now, "self financing" covers 18,700 teachers per
> month. Some teachers don't accept the money because
> they have other means; teachers only accept it if they
> need it.[9]

Before the recent troubles, a Kosovo company, which employed
some seventy-four Albanians, published school books in the Albanian
language. In 1991, the state imposed new "emergency" management,
imposed new rules, and fired sixty-one of the Albanian workers. Since
then, the publishing of Albanian-language texts has ground to a halt.[10]
According to one Albanian educator:

---

[8] Human Rights Watch/Helsinki interview in Priština, September 1993.

[9] Human Rights Watch/Helsinki interview in Priština, September 1993.

[10] See Ursula Ruston, "Where Journalism is a Crime," 21(2) *Index on Censorship*,
February 1992.

> For the past two years, not a single school book has been printed in the Albanian language. We're now using old books and books printed in Switzerland and taken across the border illegally. For example, we're printing a first grade reader in Switzerland.[11]

In addition to a shortage of books, Albanian schools suffer from a shortage of chalk, blackboards, and other basic supplies.

While Turkish children in Kosovo still attend state-sponsored Turkish elementary schools, Turkish leaders have created five "parallel" high schools, based on a structure similar to the Albanian parallel schools.[12]

UPDATE ON THE UNIVERSITY OF PRIŠTINA

Since its inception in 1970, Priština University has offered instruction in Albanian and, although classes were offered also in Serbian, the vast majority of the students until recent times were ethnic Albanian. Originally, the university had close ties to the University of Tirana (in Albania); however, after the student uprisings in Kosovo in 1981, Serbia took steps to cut off contacts between the two institutions. At the same time, the number of Albanian students enrolled each year was reduced, purportedly through a quota system and through "moral and political" fitness checks on incoming students.

In 1990, the Serbian parliament passed a law entitling all students of minority groups (i.e. non-Serbian) to higher education in the language of their mother tongue, provided that at least thirty students in the same year of studies sought the same instruction.[13] Although Mr. Božović (the Kosovo Secretary of Education) points to this measure as a victory for Albanians, few Albanians share his opinion. Instead, they argue that by requiring thirty students in each course, the law actually cuts back on educational opportunities for students of national minorities. Serbian

---

[11] Human Rights Watch/Helsinki interview in Priština, September 1993.

[12] Human Rights Watch/Helsinki interview with Sezair Shaipi in Prizren, December 1993.

[13] Serbian Law on Colleges and Universities, *Serbian Official Register*, No. 5/90.

students can receive instruction in Serbian even when fewer than thirty students are enrolled in a class.

The 1990 law, however, was far better for Albanians than a new law enacted in August 1992, which left Albanian-language instruction up to the discretion of the board of universities.[14] Since the boards are overwhelmingly Serbian, this measure virtually ensured that instruction would be provided in Serbian only.

In addition to these measures on language instruction, the Serbian parliament has controlled the University of Priština through a set of "emergency measures." Under these measures, which were first enacted in June 28, 1990, and remain in effect today, Serbian officials fired Albanian university administrators and replaced them with Serbs and Montenegrins, and reduced the number of Albanian students to the number of Serbian students — a disproportionate allocation given that ninety percent of the high school graduates in Kosovo are Albanian.[15]

In the 1991/92 school year, all university buildings were closed to Albanians, disrupting the education of some 23,000 Albanian students who had already begun their studies there. Today, the buildings are still used solely by Serbian, Montenegrin and foreign students. According to Mr. Božović, Albanian students are free to attend classes, but they have simply chosen to boycott the university in support of their leaders' larger political aims. Albanian educators and students, however, dispute this account, contending that they are blocked from the university, through the draconian, discriminatory measures that were implemented in 1991. In any event, it is clear that Albanians refuse to recognize the newly imposed Serbian university administrators and that, unless they do so, they will not be permitted to take part in the university.

The 1993/94 school year began with over 25,000 university students crammed into private homes, taught by Albanian professors who no longer work at the university. Dr. Zenel Kelmendi, the dean of the Priština "parallel" medical school, illustrated the situation:

---

[14] The Law on Universities, *Official Gazette of Serbia* 54/92, August 8, 1992. See *The Situation of Human Rights in the Former Yugoslavia*, Tadeusz Mazowiecki, Special Rapporteur of the UN Commission on Human Rights, February 10, 1993, p. 35.

[15] Interview with Independent Association of University Professors and Other Scientific Workers in Kosovo in October 1993.

A year after [the university was closed down], we
organized classes in private homes. The medical and
dentistry students now have classes in sixteen private
homes. Our staff includes 155 general practitioners, 105
specialists, seventy-one assistant professors, thirty
associate professors, thirty-eight regular professors and
three members of the Kosovo Academy of Arts and
Sciences. Our 1,864 students practice in private clinics.

One of our biggest problems is that we can't get corpses
so our students have to go to Albania to study
anatomy.[16]   Also, the police harass the students and
professors. They interrupted entrance exams this year
[1993/94 school year], so we had to hold it secretly
several days later.[17]

Numerous professors attested that they had been fired from their
positions but, according to Mr. Božović, most of them had left voluntarily
because they refused to accept the new "emergency measures."[18]
According to Albanian sources, over 900 Albanian professors and other
instructors from the university are now living off welfare payments from
"solidarity funds," or through donations from family members living
abroad."

STATUS OF NEGOTIATIONS OVER SCHOOLS

As of this writing, negotiations over Kosovo schools are headed
nowhere. The situation looked more promising in the middle of 1992,
when the London Peace Conference on the Former Yugoslavia
established a special working group on Kosovo and took up the issue of

---

[16] This is no longer possible because of the travel restrictions imposed by the
Serbian authorities. See "Introduction" to this report.

[17] Human Rights Watch/Helsinki interview in Priština, November 1993.

[18] The minister said that the university still had twenty-nine Albanian
professors, a figure that Albanian educational leaders dispute.

education. The group met on several occasions in 1992 and the
beginning of 1993; however, no progress was made on the key issue of
who should have authority over Kosovo schools — local Albanians or
Belgrade Serbs. As the 1993/94 school year began, both sides were very
pessimistic.

Formally, the problem concerns a conflict over educational
programs. Mr. Božović said that if the teachers recognized the new,
centralized education system, they would be paid by the state and all
Albanian students would be allowed back into the schools. However, Mr.
Osmani the Albanian educator, argues that in his opinion the educational
program is not the true essence of the problem:

> The real problem is that Serbia wants to force Albanians
> to recognize the government in Belgrade. Serbia wants
> to force us to accept the sovereignty of Serbia over
> Kosovo and over education.[19]

In the view of Mr. Osmani and other Albanian leaders, the Serbian
government's removal of Kosovo's autonomy, by constitutional
amendment in 1990, was unconstitutional and thus constituted a legal
break in the province's links with Serbia. Education, he contends, has
become a pawn in Serbia's struggle to annex Kosovo illegally.

Serbian leaders, on the other hand, argue that the 1990
constitutional amendments legally reintegrated Kosovo into Serbia. It is
the Albanians who are using the issue of education, argues Mr. Božović,
not the Serbs. According to him, the Albanians use schools to brainwash
their children:

> They bring up their children with separatist ideas. The
> next stage, they teach them, is to merge with Albania. ...
> We've seen translations of their programs. They teach
> only Albanian language, history and traditions, nothing
> Serbian. They even print their own books on Rome and
> bring them in. ... And, in history classes, according to the
> Albanian program, the fifth grade text says that Serbia

---

[19] Human Rights Watch/Helsinki interview in Priština, September 1993.

occupied Kosovo.   In Geography classes, they give Albanian names to all of the towns.[20]

Rexhep Osmani, the head of the Albanian Teachers Association, vehemently disagrees:

> They try to accuse us of trying to form a Republic of Kosova through the school system. This isn't true. We just want independence for our schools, like we had before. Serbia wants to decide the structure of schools, the number of schools, the educational programs, and the appointment of directors to run the schools. If we allow that, what kind of independence can we have?[21]

Mr. Božović says that he "still wants to reach negotiation, but the plans must be verified and signed in Belgrade." According to the minister, "the sticking point at negotiations is that they want Kosovo to be a republic; now Kosovo is part of Serbia." But, he assures, "we want children to go back to school."

However, Mr. Osmani doesn't believe that the education minister had any intention of negotiating a fair settlement on the schools:

> I've met personally with Danilo Marković, the education minister, about ten times. They're been totally dishonest with us. For example, when I met with the Serbian government in September 1991, nine months after they had closed the high schools, the first thing Kosutić (the former vice-president of the Serbian government) said is, "We won't touch the universities." Then they closed the universities. I understand that Serbia has notified the U.N. that they've established contact with us. They say that "dialogue" has started. But this isn't any real dialogue![22]

---

[20] Human Rights Watch/Helsinki interview in Priština, September 1993.

[21] Human Rights Watch/Helsinki interview in Priština, September 1993.

[22] Human Rights Watch/Helsinki interview in Priština, September 1993.

According to Mr. Osmani, Serbia "keeps students hostage by demanding that laws and procedures be applied in Kosovo that have been brought into force illegally and without our agreement. We never imagined that we would be in this position, especially for so long. We thought that international intervention could help solve things."

On September 9, 1993, negotiations broke off completely when the Serbs refused to meet any longer in Geneva, insisting that all future talks be held in Belgrade.[23] This, however, was utterly unacceptable to the Albanians.

RECENT CASES OF HARASSMENT OF ALBANIAN TEACHERS AND FACULTY

Albanian teachers and students participating in the "parallel" educational system are, according to Mr. Osmani, "under constant pressure from violence, and tension as a result of violence." As one teacher, Bashkim Syla, lamented at the beginning of the 1993/94 school year: "This is the third year for us at this school. Things have only gotten worse. ... Now we have a lot of problems with police harassment."

Mr. Božović flatly denied all of the allegations of police harassment of school teachers, claiming:

> Police never go near the schools. It is not true that teachers have been harassed and detained. If it ever happens that a police officer takes a teacher away from a classroom, it is for something else, not for teaching.[24]

Human Rights Watch/Helsinki, however, has collected scores of statements from teachers and students harassed by the police that belie these claims. For example, at the end of the last school year, around

---

[23] See Fabian Schmidt, "Has the Kosovo Crisis Been Internationalized?" Vo. 2, No. 44, Radio Free Europe/Radio Liberty *Research Report*, November 1993.

[24] Human Rights Watch/Helsinki interview in Priština, September 1993.

June 17, the director of an Albanian high school[25] that was situated in
a private home in Priština was beaten and arrested. According to one
witnesses, M.X.:

> He was beaten very badly. He was beaten professionally.
> By the time they were done, he had a hard time holding
> a pen. He was beaten not only at the school but again at
> the police station, where they took him by force. After
> they were done, they dumped him in front of the police
> station. The next day, even though he could hardly walk,
> he came to see us at the school to show us what they did.
> His hands and feet were black and swollen [demonstrates
> how he was beaten on the soles of his feet so that he had
> to walk on the edges of his feet]. After he left, the police
> came here looking for him. They said, "We know that
> he's here." He wasn't here, but they harassed us anyway,
> looking through everything, disrupting us, threatening
> us."[26]

Nexhip Aliu, another teacher at the same school, added:

> Last school year, the police came in this area looking for
> the school. They know we have a school here, so they
> were going down the street, saying that they were
> looking for someone else. I went out to see what was
> going on. They asked me where the house of so-and-so
> was. I said "I don't know. This is not an information
> service." Two policemen handcuffed me. They said,
> "How come you don't know where his house is?" They

---

[25] At this school there are 1,500 students; they attend school in three shifts,
from 8 A.M. to 12 P.M.; 12 P.M. to 3 P.M.; and 3:15 P.M. until 6:30 P.M.; there are sixty
teachers. Most of the high school students are girls; many of the boys have left
Kosovo to avoid the draft or to earn money abroad for their families. The
graduation rate is high: seventy to eighty percent in all high schools. The state
of Albania recognizes these private schools and their diplomas. In addition,
students have gone from these schools to schools in Germany and the U.S.

[26] Human Rights Watch/Helsinki interview in Priština, September 1993.

knew that he was the host of the school. They hit me in
front of my mother and wife with their fists. One of
them cocked his rifle and stood five meters away from
me, pointing it at me, threatening to kill me. They said,
"Why do you let your children stay here? When we come
next time, we won't let you leave so soon."[27]

Also at the end of last school year, Mr. Aliu said:

On June 16 or 17, 1993, three plainclothes police officers
came to this house and entered this room [the room
serving as a "faculty lounge"] They said, "What are you
doing here?" We said, "We're teachers." They wanted
our IDs, our documentation and harassed us. They went
to two classrooms and took two class logs. I didn't ask
for a warrant; that gets you into more trouble. The
officers ordered us to go with them to the station. There
were too many of us to fit into their car, so they ordered
one student to drive us in our car. They took his I.D. to
force him to obey. When we got to the police station
they immediately released us. We still haven't gotten the
classroom logs back.

The principle of an Albanian high school, Abdyl Gashi,
remembered another incident from the previous school year:

On September 12, 1992, the police came to my house in
the morning and detained me for three to four hours
and beat me badly. First, they talked about education
and alleged that the work of their school is illegal. Then
a plainclothes officer came, and acted very nice. He
shook my hand and said, "Hello, you're the director."
Then he started beating me. They beat me for about
twenty to thirty minutes. I said, "Fine, beat me." During
this time, two other police stood on the sides of the room
watching. They eventually began to hit me, too. They

---

[27] Human Rights Watch/Helsinki interview in Priština, September 1993.

hit me on the head, especially on the top. I was sitting
down at this time. I didn't faint, but I couldn't stand up
either. The police said to me, "Go to your colleagues and
tell them what we did to you."[28]

Professor Nexhat Daci teaches chemistry at the "parallel" medical
school of the university. He recounted:

Last June, we were holding a chemistry exam in a house
in Vranjevac [a part of Priština]. All of a sudden, four of
five policemen armed to the teeth barged into the room.
They took away all our material and took six of us
professors and the owner of the house to the police
station. They held us for several hours. They were
asking me about the university: who finances it, how is it
organized, etc. They insulted us a lot. They also said
"What [they] did in Bosnia is child's play compared to
what [they] will do here." But, they didn't beat any of
us.[29]

Frequently, police take students into the station for "informative
talks," a practice that began in September 1990. According to one
teacher at another Albanian high school in Priština:

Usually they ask the students, "Where do you go to
school? Who is your teacher, your principal? Do you
recognize Serbia?" Sometimes they just keep the child
for a while and frighten him, but sometimes they also
beat him up a bit. We've had cases in which they've
begun by really beating them badly, and then asking
questions.[30]

---

[28] Human Rights Watch/Helsinki interview in Priština, September 1993.

[29] Human Rights Watch/Helsinki interview in Priština, November 1993.

[30] Human Rights Watch/Helsinki interview in Priština, September 1993.

In addition to such physical harassment, Albanian teachers and professors complain that Serbian authorities have prevented them from traveling abroad to participate in academic conferences and other exchanges. This dilemma has particularly hampered the ability of Albanian scientists to keep up with recent developments and has hindered instruction in the sciences.

THE STATUS OF HEALTH CARE

UPDATE ON MASS LAYOFFS OF ALBANIAN
HEALTH CARE PROFESSIONALS

In July and August 1990, Kosovo health care was placed under Serbian "emergency management." Almost immediately, Albanian physicians, nurses, technicians and other health care personnel were laid off en masse.[1] Among the reasons given by Serbian authorities for the dismissals was the purported refusal of Albanian doctors to recognize the new management and to abide by their orders; another justification was the alleged mistreatment by Albanian health care workers of Serbian patients. According to the Kosovo Ministry of Health, Albanian doctors had started to use their positions to advocate for a greater Albania.

Dr. Radomir Božović, the Kosovo health minister, gave Human Rights Watch/Helsinki his version of the firings of 1990 as follows:

> In 1990, propaganda entered hospitals that prevented doctors from doing their job. For example, they spread the rumor that someone had poisoned Albanian children. A commission of experts looked into this and found absolutely no evidence. It was all made up. ... At this time, patients that needed treatment were not let in by [Albanian] doctors. This forced the government to enact special measures on health care. After this, a number of doctors left their jobs of their own free will. Others ignored the new management and eventually were fired. In some hospitals, doctors were asked to sign a paper recognizing the state of Serbia. This was the doing of the management. State officials insisted that this shouldn't be done.[2]

---

[1] For further information, see The International Helsinki Federation, *The Health Care Situation in Kosovo*, October 1991; Helsinki Watch, *Yugoslavia: Human Rights Abuses in Kosovo 1990-1992*, October 1992, pg. 42-43.

[2] Human Rights Watch/Helsinki interview in Priština, September 1993.

According to the minister, anyone fired for refusing to sign an oath can appeal and get his job back.

Albanian health care professionals, however, describe a quite different scenario:. According to Dr. Zenel Kelmendi, dean of the Medical School of Priština University (the "parallel" university):

> The problems started after the 1981 demonstrations. We had about 145 wounded and many dead. We doctors worked around the clock to help all of the wounded, both demonstrators and police. Two or three days later, the wounded policemen were flown to Belgrade, Skopje and Niš for treatment. The regime claimed that we had been preparing for this for years because the hospitals were so well organized. They arrested and interrogated many of the hospital personnel. Eight doctors were sentenced to up to eight years in prison.[3]

According to Dr. Kelmendi, the repression of Albanian health care professionals was triggered by their opposition to Kosovo's losing its autonomy in the late 1980s:

> Two hundred and sixteen intellectuals from Kosovo, including over a hundred doctors, wrote a letter to Serbia's Assembly demanding that it reconsider the decision to end Kosovo's autonomy. This angered the Serbian regime and they accused us of betrayal.
>
> A few days later, three armored personnel carriers (APCs) full of policemen stormed the clinics, arresting doctors, knocking everything down. Three doctors — Dr.

---

[3] Human Rights Watch/Helsinki interview in Priština, November 1993. Dr Kelmendi added that, "In March of 1989 there was a mass poisoning of Albanian children. A commission arrived from Belgrade. They at first confirmed that this really was a poisoning and later denied it." *Id.* See also Helsinki Watch, *Yugoslavia: Human Rights Abuses in Kosovo 1990-1992* (October 1992), pp. 43-44. According to Dr. Radomir Božović, the Kosovo minister of health, no one has ever successfully proved that the poisoning was intentional. Human Rights Watch/Helsinki interview in Priština, September 1993.

Ali Zatriqi, Dr. Ymer Aliu and Dr. Shefki Goxhufi — were handcuffed and arrested. Terrified, most patients walked out of the hospital. We were later accused of kicking out patients, but we had no time to stop them.[4]

This event apparently precipitated the mass firings of Albanian health care personnel:

Serbian doctors were appointed directors of the clinics [in place of Albanian directors]. Meanwhile, the authorities put up on a lamppost outside the clinic a list of thirty names of Albanian doctors who were not allowed to enter the hospital. Thirty-eight Serbian doctors took our places. They all carried pistols. The Serbian regime imposed emergency measures and most Albanian doctors and personnel were fired.[5]

Doctors and nurses who were out on maternity leave at this time were later allowed to return to work (see below).

UPDATE ON "PARALLEL HEALTH CARE"

Serbian law officially allows for the operation of private health care facilities that are properly registered pursuant to the relevant regulations. According to many Albanian physicians, however, permits for private institutions are issued in a highly selective and discriminatory manner. Clinics are in continuous danger of being closed by Serbian authorities, and their staffs in danger of being harassed and detained by police.

Dr. Radomir Božović, the Kosovo minister of health, denies any problem with "parallel" health clinics:

There are no private hospitals in this province, but there are 250 private facilities dealing with health; ninety percent are owned by Albanians. There is not a similar

---

[4] Human Rights Watch/Helsinki interview in Priština, November 1993.

[5] Human Rights Watch/Helsinki in Priština, November 1993.

problem as with education. Based on our survey of
patients, we know that only a small percentage of
patients use private facilities, only those with enough
money to pay." He admitted that there may be some
unregistered private facilities but, he contended, "it is not
a big number, so we overlook them."[6]

In the fall of 1993, Human Rights Watch/Helsinki visited a
handful of private clinics operated by Albanians, some of which were
licensed and some of which were operating illegally. All of the clinics are
organized on a voluntary basis, with a staff of general practice physicians,
specialists and nurses. All of the clinics report that they provide services
for free when the patients do not have the ability to pay.

A clinic visited in Mitrovica, provides a good illustration of the
operations of private Albanian clinics. Mitrovica, a mining town in which
12,000 workers have been dismissed from the mines and are without
health insurance, has been hit particularly hard.   Human Rights
Watch/Helsinki visited a storefront clinic that provides care to about 130
people per day, mostly for free. The health care professionals at the
clinic tend to ailments and minor emergencies, referring patients to the
hospital for more complicated procedures. Although the quarters are
cramped and the medical equipment is old and breaking, the facilities
appear clean, and patients appear satisfied with the care they receive
there.

Doctors at the clinic report difficulty in obtaining a license to
officially registered and to obtain a more suitable flat. According to one
of the head physicians: "The authorities come and control this place.
They try to close us because we don't have a license. We are working
very hard to not be closed."[7]

The doctors at the clinic pointed to the delivery and care of
newborn children as their greatest dilemma.   All of the doctors
interviewed emphasized that the percentage of newborn deaths has
increased dramatically. "The main reason for this increase," one doctor
explained, "is that women do not have proper access to prenatal care and

---

[6] Human Rights Watch/Helsinki in Priština, September 1993.

[7] Human Rights Watch/Helsinki interview in Mitrovica, September 1993.
Identity of person withheld for protection.

proper nutrition and medical care during pregnancy."[8] Other problems
in providing health care at private clinics include: shortages of vaccines,
lack of incubators, no access to surgical equipment and a scarcity of
sterile supplies.[9]

THE DETERIORATING QUALITY OF HEALTH IN KOSOVO

Care in Hospitals

M.R. is one of the few Albanian nurses who was on leave during
the purges of Albanian health care workers and thus she was allowed to
return to work when her leave expired.   When she returned to the
hospital, M.R. was shocked at how much had changed:

> We were forced to write in Serbian, in the Cyrillic
> alphabet. I refused and I am one of the few who have
> not written a word in Serbian over the past three years.
> Still I was not fired. This only proves how they need us
> in the hospital. ... [Unlike before,] there are no private
> contacts between the Serbian and Albanian staff. We
> never even drink our coffees together as we used to
> before. ... Doctors accept bribes because their salaries are
> so low. The authorities used to give Serbian doctors and
> hospital staff potatoes and meat, as a supplement to their
> salaries. Now they do not get even that.[10]

M.R. described horrible conditions for patients at the hospitals:

> Patients have to provide their own infusions, bandages,
> antiseptics, medicines. ... When an emergency case is

---

[8] Human Rights Watch/Helsinki interview in Mitrovica, September 1993.
Identity of person withheld for protection.

[9] Human Rights Watch/Helsinki interview with physicians in Mitrovica,
Uroševac, and Priština, September - October 1993.

[10] Human Rights Watch/Helsinki interview in Priština, November 1993.
Identity of person withheld for protection.

brought in, the first person to visit the patient gets
charged for all of his expenses. There is no heating in
the rooms. The food is terrible. Patients get only tea for
breakfast and rice and potatoes for lunch and dinner.
Families have to bring them food.

Only those who can afford operations get operated on.
About ninety-five percent of the hospital patients are
Albanians because they have no other place to go. Since
the conditions are still better in Serbian hospitals [outside
Kosovo], most Serbian patients get transferred there.
The Serbian doctors also try to get jobs somewhere in
Serbia proper so only very young doctors, those who
cannot choose where they work, still work in Kosovo.
Often a mere trainee operates in complicated cases. It
doesn't seem to matter if the patient lives or dies.[11]

This description has been confirmed by visits to Kosovo hospitals
by Human Rights Watch/Helsinki and other independent monitoring
groups. Similarly, Q.M., another Albanian doctor who had been on
maternity leave during the purges and allowed to return to work, also
described deteriorating work conditions at her hospital:

The relations among the workers [are] still very tense
and obedience [is] valued more than knowledge. There
is a lot of corruption and bribes among doctors....I have
had a lot of problems over the past two years. I raised
the question of some very sophisticated hospital
equipment suddenly disappearing. They told me that it
was being repaired in Belgrade. No one had a list of
what was sent to Belgrade. The equipment never
returned to the hospital. Three other machines, each of
which costs 70,000 deutsche marks, are "being repaired"
in Skopje since 1990. I am sure that all of this
equipment is now being used in a private [Serbian] clinic.
A mother of six children died at the ward and I insisted

---

[11] Human Rights Watch/Helsinki interview in Priština, November 1993.
Identity of person withheld for protection.

that this happened due to malpractice. It turned out that
I was right, but no one was even reprimanded in the
matter.[12]

After several disputes with the chief doctor over the provision of health
care, Q.M. was fired on October 6, 1993 for "obstructing work."

In addition to the problems in hospitals described above, Albanian
and Serbian doctors alike report a lack of all kinds of drugs, sterile
supplies, diagnostic materials and hepatitis and HIV blood tests for blood
transfusions. Moreover, in order to save time and money, patients are
being sent home too early after operations.

Status of Health Care Generally[13]

The mortality rate for Kosovo is deceptively low, at 5.4 (figure
per 1,000 people in population), because the population is quite young
(fifty-two percent of the population is under age nineteen; the average
age of men is 23.9, of women 24.5.). Still, according to Dr. Radomir
Božović, the Kosovo minister of health, the death rate for all members of
the population has increased due to malnutrition and disease. Many of
the recent cases of death, Dr. Božović said, are due to ailments that would
have formerly been treatable, and due to an outbreak of diseases which
formerly had occurred only at a very low rate, such as polio and
tuberculosis.[14]

The mortality rate of newborns in particular has escalated in the
past two years, as the following chart, drawn from the Kosovo minister
of health, indicates:

---

[12] Human Rights Watch/Helsinki interview in Priština, November 1993.
Identity of person withheld for protection.

[13] All information contained herein is from the (Parallel) University of Priština
Medical School for 1993 and an interview with the Kosovo minister of health, Dr.
Radomir Božović, in Priština, September 1993. When there is a disparity
between the sources, the source of the data is noted.

[14] Human Rights Watch/Helsinki interview in Priština, September 1993.

Mortality Rate of Newborns

Date	Number of deaths in first year (per 1,000 births)
1954	143
1990	38.4
1992(estimate)	50

Kosovo has a very high birth rate, the highest in Europe. In 1990, official government statistics (which do not count many home births) recorded 55,000 births. Officials fear that the infant mortality rate, which is about 5.5 percent, is rising due to lack of proper medical care. According to one Albanian physician, few women receive prenatal care and high risk pregnancies are rarely detected.

Official statistics indicate that thirteen women died in childbirth in 1990. The Kosovo secretary of health was worried that this number could be on the rise, because, since 1990, the number of hospital births has declined as more women are choosing to have births at home or in clinics. The reason for this trend, he guesses, is the increasing inability of people to pay for hospital services, and Albanian mistrust of Serb-run hospitals.

Medical care for children has been crippled by a serious shortage of vaccines. The Kosovo ministry of health estimates that the vaccination rate for children has dropped from a high of ninety percent in 1990 to less that fifty percent in 1992. Due to a generally poor standard of living and a lack of preventative medical care, school children are beset by a host of ailments. The University of Priština Medical School estimated that in 1993, fifty percent of the school children had lice, and twelve to twenty percent had scabies. In 1992, there were 200,000 registered cases of scabies.[15] And in 1992, 221 children died of enterocolitis, a disease associated with poverty. Between 1983 and 1990, doctors in Kosovo reported no cases of children with polio. Yet, from 1990-1993 there were twenty cases.[16]

---

[15] University of Priština Medical School for 1993.

[16] Human Rights Watch/Helsinki interview with Dr. Kelmendi, (Parallel) University of Priština Medical School, in Priština, November 1993. According to Dr. Kelmendi, each child with polio is a threat to 1,000 others.

The population density in Kosovo — 197.3 per square kilometer — is the second highest in Europe. Only forty-six percent of the Kosovo population drink tap water, and only 28.9 percent of the households and thirty-three percent of the inhabitants are linked to sewage systems.[17] Albanian leaders reported that although they had set up parallel education systems and hospital systems, they did not have the resources to deal with sewers and other problems of the Kosovo infrastructure.

The Kosovo minister of health blames the bleak picture on the international sanctions that have been imposed against Serbia. Albanian health care professionals, however, generally support the sanctions, pointing out that the deterioration in health care in Kosovo began long before the sanctions had been put in place.[18]

---

[17] (Parallel) University of Priština Medical School for 1993.

[18] Food and medicines are among the items exempt from the U.N. trade embargo on Serbia and Montenegro, but approval for some humanitarian aid needs to go through bureaucratic approval by the UN Sanctions Committee.

VIOLATIONS OF INTERNATIONAL LAW

The treatment of Albanians described above demonstrates that Serbia has failed to guarantee ethnic minorities equality and nondiscrimination, in violation of its own law, as well as of the principles clearly set forth in the International Covenant on Civil and Political Rights (ICCPR), the Helsinki Final Act and subsequent Conference on Security and Cooperation in Europe (CSCE) Conferences on the Human Dimension in Copenhagen (1990), Paris (1990), Cracow (1991) and Geneva (1991). In particular, among other violations of international human rights laws and principles, Human Rights Watch/Helsinki emphasizes the following:

- The police brutality and abuse in detention described above violates Articles 6 and 7 of the International Covenant on Civil and Political Rights (ICCPR), the U.N. Basic Principles on the Use of Firearms by Law Enforcement Officials, the U.N. Code of Conduct for Law Enforcement Officials,[1] the U.N. Body of Principles for the Protection of All Persons Under Any Form of Detention and Imprisonment,[2] the U.N. Standard Minimum Rules for the Treatment of Prisoners (and Procedures for Effective Implementation of the Rules), and the Convention Against Torture and Other Cruel, Inhuman or Degrading Treatment or Punishment;

- The arbitrary arrests and cases of detainment are in contradiction to Article 9 of the ICCPR, which holds that "[n]o one shall be subject to arbitrary arrest or detention" and that "[n]o one shall be deprived of his liberty except on such grounds and in accordance with such procedures as are established by international law;"

---

[1] General Assembly of the United Nations, Resolution 34/169, December 17, 1979.

[2] General Assembly Resolution of the United Nations in Resolution 43/173, December 9, 1988.

135

• The cases in which the accused are in fact detained solely on account of non-violent expression of political views is a violation of Article 19 of the ICCPR, which declares that "everyone shall have the right to freedom of expression;"

• The restrictions on the freedom of association violate Articles 21 and 22 of the ICCPR, which protect the rights to "assembly" and "association;" Article II, Section 9.2 of the Concluding Document of the Copenhagen Meeting of the Conference on the Human Dimension of the Conference on Security and Cooperation in Europe (CSCE),[3] which affirms that "everyone shall have the right to peaceful assembly and demonstration;" and The Charter of Paris which similarly recognizes the right to "freedom of association and peaceful assembly;"[4]

• The banning of or interference with the Albanian press violates Article 19 of the ICCPR, which grants the media freedom to "impart information," declaring that "everyone shall have the right to freedom of expression" as well as Article 27 which provides that members belonging to ethnic minorities shall have a right "to enjoy their own culture" and "use their own language;"

• Unwarranted raids on and searches of houses violate Article 17 of the ICCPR, which states that "no one shall be subjected to arbitrary or unlawful interference with his privacy, family, home...;"

• The denial of a fair trial and other due process guarantees violates Articles 9 and 14 of the ICCPR (as noted above), as well as the CSCE Vienna Concluding Document (Section 13.9); and the Copenhagen Concluding Document (Section 5.16);

• Employment discrimination on the basis of ethnicity and political belief, including the mass layoffs of Albanian health care professionals, educators, and other workers, violates the

---

[3] Yugoslavia signed the CSCE document in June 1990.

[4] Yugoslavia signed the Charter of Paris in November 1990.

International Labor Organization Convention Concerning Discrimination in Respect of Employment and Occupation; and

- The harassment, detention and interrogation of local and international human rights groups violates not only the freedom of the press and of association but also Principle VII of the CSCE Final Act which allows for monitoring a state's internal human rights situation.

RECOMMENDATIONS

TO THE GOVERNMENT OF SERBIA

Human Rights Watch/Helsinki calls upon the Serbian government to abide by its obligations under international and national law to protect the human rights of ethnic Albanians and other non-Serbs, specifically in the following respects:

Police Violence and Abuse in Detention

• Enact legislation, issue and follow published guidelines that strictly control the use of force by police or by the military in Kosovo, along the following lines: the standard for the use of lethal force should be "absolute necessity;" the force should be in proportion to the actual danger; and civilians aggrieved under such guidelines should be allowed legal redress;

• Cease all police and military activity aimed at forcibly removing non-Serbs from their homes; allow all those who have been forced to leave their homes the opportunity to return without fear of reprisals or harassment;

• Return the homes and property illegally confiscated from civilians in an expedited manner;

• Investigate and punish police and security officers responsible for treating Albanians in detention in an inhuman manner, for using torture against them and other force intended to coerce "confessions;"

• Investigate and punish police and security officials responsible for use of undue force against Albanian civilians in the context of street and house arrests and interrogations;

• Investigate and prosecute those responsible for raids on towns in northern Kosovo and elsewhere in attempts to push Albanians from their homes and to otherwise harass or intimidate the villagers;

• Take steps to end random street stops and searches and to ensure that all searches are conducted without degrading or harassing measures; and

• Require a warrant (made out in advance) for entering a private residence or business and for examining and seizing documents.

Freedom of Association, Speech and the Press

• Allow persons to assemble freely at peaceful gatherings including meetings which are aimed at criticizing the Serbian government or Serbian rule in Kosovo;

• Immediately cease the harassment, interrogation and arrest of individuals who meet with or aid foreign delegations;

• Immediately cease the harassment, interrogation and arrest of individuals who investigate human rights abuses in Kosovo;

• Allow workers to organize in independent trade unions and recognize them as parties to collective bargaining;

• Guarantee the free expression and not threaten the preservation and development of Albanian culture and language, as well as Turkish and Muslim culture and language;

• Respect the freedom of speech and expression of all persons and organizations in Kosovo in line with international guarantees;

• Respect the freedom of the press in Kosovo, including the Albanian-language media; allow journalists to report freely without fear of reprisal; and

• Lift the ban on and cease interference with the Albanian-language publications *Rilindja*, *Zeri*, and other non-Serbian publications.

Manipulation of the Legal System and the Right to a Fair Trial

• Repeal all laws which discriminate against Albanians and lift
  "special" and/or "emergency" measures in Kosovo, both legally
  and in practice;

• Reinstate an independent judiciary with respect for due process
  and the rule of law;

• Reappoint Albanian judges who had been fired for their ethnicity
  and political beliefs;

• Drop all charges against those who have been indicted for the
  peaceful expression of opinion or for membership in a group
  which is banned or looked upon unfavorably by the Serbian
  government; and refrain from making arrests on such grounds;

• Drop all pending and future charges based solely on material
  discovered in searches without warrants;

• Drop all pending and future charges based solely on "confessions"
  extracted by force;

• Accord due process to all persons detained and/or accused of
  crimes, including Albanians accused of "violating the territorial
  integrity of Yugoslavia" or other "terrorist" activities;

• Inform all detainees immediately of the grounds for arrest and
  any charges against them;

• Provide all detainees with immediate and regular access to
  attorneys; accord all detainees with the right to petition for
  review of their detention without undue delay;

• Allow all detainees time and facilities for the preparation for a
  defense and the ability to communicate with counsel;

• Guarantee trial without unreasonable delay before a competent,
  independent tribunal;

- Grant the accused the right to be present at trial as well as the right to remain silent and not to be compelled to testify against oneself; and

- Provide compensation for unlawful arrest or detention.

The Militarization of Kosovo

- Prosecute individuals, members of paramilitary groups, and the police who carry arms in an unlawful manner, terrorizing other civilians and, at times, beating, shooting and killing them;

- Lift travel restrictions for Albanians, return illegally confiscated passports and issue passports to former political prisoners;

- Collect all arms illegally distributed to civilians in Kosovo, and take steps to prevent the future distribution of weapons to civilians, including Serbs and Montenegrins, in Kosovo; and

- Investigate Yugoslav army recruits and officers responsible for use of undue force against Albanian civilians, including those responsible for the wounding and the death of Albanian civilians as described above.

Education, Employment and Health Care

- Immediately cease the harassment, beatings and interrogations of Albanian educators and school children;

- License private health care clinics on a non-discriminatory basis, and refrain from unwarranted and discriminatory interference with their operations;

- Support renewed negotiations over the education system of Kosovo in a neutral setting, under the purvey of a neutral moderator;

- Provide education to Albanian, Turkish and Muslim children in a non-discriminatory manner which provides due respect to the students' language and culture;

- Provide health care to all residents of Kosovo on a non-discriminatory basis, in line with international standards.

- Reinstate all of those unlawfully dismissed from their jobs because of ethnic or political affiliation;

- Reinstate those dismissed from their jobs for refusal to sign loyalty oaths;

- Take steps to correct and prevent the intentional and state-induced social and economic marginalization of ethnic Albanians; and

- Immediately cease undue interference with and disruption of distribution of humanitarian aid to Kosovo Albanians.

The Right to Monitor

- Cease all interference with the work of local and international human rights monitors; and

- Allow the immediate reinstatement of international monitoring missions in Kosovo.

TO THE INTERNATIONAL COMMUNITY

Human Rights Watch/Helsinki calls on the United Nations and the CSCE to take immediate steps to re-establish a long-term human rights monitoring mission throughout the Federal Republic of Yugoslavia, including Kosovo. The United States and all other nations concerned about protecting human rights should, visibly and vocally, support such efforts. Moreover, as a first step, the U.N. and all nations of the world should demand that Serbia abide by international human rights standards in Kosovo. If Serbia does not comply, the U.N. should immediately explore all options for a peaceful solution in Kosovo, one that stems the tide of violence without sacrificing the human rights of any ethnic or political group.

APPENDIX A
Text of May 28, 1993 Letter to Serbian President Slobodon Milošević

May 28, 1993

His Excellency Slobodon Milošević
President of the Republic of Serbia
Marsala Tita 14
11000 Belgrade
SERBIA

Dear President Milošević:

Helsinki Watch, a division of Human Rights Watch, has learned that the Serbian authorities have closed down the publishing house "Rilindja" and all Albanian-language mass media in the province of Kosovo. On May 21, the publishing house "Rilindja" was renamed "Panorama" and a new management appointed by the Serbian Parliament on May 24. The new management has informed all employees to sign loyalty oaths by May 28 or be dismissed.

Helsinki Watch has further learned of the November 1992 law adopted by the Serbian Parliament which explicitly called for "Rilindja" to be renamed and all its activities, including its publishing policy, be re-organized and put under control of the Serbian government.

The closing of the publishing house "Rilindja" is a serious manifestation of a larger pattern of repression of the Albanians in Kosovo which Helsinki Watch described in its report entitled *Yugoslavia: Human Rights Abuses in Kosovo 1990-1992*. It is also a culmination of the process of denying the Albanians the right to free press and free expression which in the past included:

- Closing down of the newspaper *Rilindja*
- Banning of the political journal *Zeri*
- Banning of the weekly magazine *Bota e Re*
- Banning of the weekly newspaper *Dielli*
- Harassment and imprisonment of journalists

In protest against the latest action by the Serbian government, Mr. Adem Demaci, a chairman of the Priština-based Council for the Defense of Human Rights and Freedoms and an editor-in-chief of the weekly *Zeri*, went on hunger strike on May 24, 1993. Many others have joined Mr. Demaci in his action.

Helsinki Watch is deeply concerned with and condemns the abrogation of the right to free press and free expression in Kosovo. We are also concerned for the health and personal well-being of Mr. Demaci and his colleagues. We urge you to rescind your policies, re-open the publishing house "Rilindja" and restore freedom of the press and expression in Kosovo.

Sincerely,

Jeri Laber
Executive Director

APPENDIX B
Text of October 21, 1993 Letter to U.N. Secretary General Boutros Boutros-Ghali

October 21, 1993

Hon. Boutros Boutros-Ghali
Secretary General
United Nations
New York, NY 10017

Dear Mr. Secretary General:

Police beatings, unwarranted arrests, and abuse of Albanian civilians in detention have escalated in Kosovo since Serbia expelled the Kosovo CSCE monitoring mission in July 1993. Presently, police in Kosovo do as they please, wholly without scrutiny of any long-term, international human rights monitors. Yugoslavia flatly denied the UN Special Rapporteur on the former Yugoslavia permission to open an office in the country to monitor human rights abuses and, in July 1993, rejected UN representatives' visa applications to the region.

To abate rising police terror in Kosovo, Helsinki Watch, a division of Human Rights Watch, urges the United Nations to condemn the growing human rights violations in Kosovo, and to take immediate steps to protest the expulsion and ensure the re-employment of long-term human rights monitors in the region.

Although the Yugoslav government has greatly restricted international human rights groups' access to Kosovo, Helsinki Watch was able to conduct a mission to Kosovo in September through October 1993. Based on its own extensive interviews with witnesses and victims, Helsinki Watch has concluded that Serbian police abuse of Albanian civilians has not only continued unabated, but in fact has increased markedly over the past three months.

Particular targets of Serbian police include Albanians with former military experience, Albanian political leaders and human rights activists, and all Albanians who meet with or aid visiting delegations. Police have detained, interrogated and beaten several Albanians who aided the CSCE missions. Similarly, police arrested at least four people who met with Helsinki Watch within twenty-four hours of their meeting.

Helsinki Watch has documented numerous recent cases of grave abuse in detention, including one case in which police beat a prisoner to death. Police routinely beat and torture their prisoners, from Albanian high school principals operating within the "parallel" Albanian education system, to Albanians conducting elections for the LDK (the Democratic League of Kosovo, the leading Albanian party), to Albanian athletes playing in table tennis tournaments not sanctioned by the Serbian-controlled sports federation.

In addition to daily abuse of individual civilians, police have conducted massive raids on Albanian villages lying on the so-called "ethnic border" between Albanian villages and Serbian villages in northern Kosovo. Helsinki Watch visited some of these villages and interviewed families about five such raids. All people independently interviewed spoke of similar scenarios: ·100 to 200 police officers swarm the small villages, raiding and searching houses under the pretext of looking for weapons, severely beating civilians, and arresting a handful of men, who are later interrogated and beaten at the police station. Several of those interviewed said that police shouted, "go back to Albania where you belong," and threatened to kill them if they remained in their homes.

Helsinki Watch is also alarmed by an apparent increase in paramilitary activity, particularly in border areas. In more than one case, civilians described police working in concert with irregular troops. Helsinki Watch also documented one recent case in which two Yugoslav soldiers opened machine gun fire on two young Albanian men near the unmarked border with Macedonia, killing one and seriously wounding the other. From its own investigation of the incident, Helsinki Watch has concluded that the Albanians were a considerable distance from the border when shot, and that the soldiers fired without warning and continued to shoot after the men had fallen down.

Helsinki Watch will release a special report on Kosovo, presenting these findings on police abuse and other human rights violations, including excerpts from testimony collected. In sum, as police violence as escalated since the CSCE withdrawal, the findings only further illustrate the importance of re-establishing an international presence in the region. Thus, Helsinki Watch urges the United Nations to take immediate steps to re-employ long-term international monitors in Kosovo.

Sincerely,

Jeri Laber
Executive Director

cc: Members of the United Nations Security Council